What people are saying about

UNSINKABLE FAITH

"*Unsinkable Faith* is a powerful book to help you have a better brain and a better life."

Daniel G. Amen, MD, author of *The Brain Warrior's Way*

"When life has beaten you down, *Unsinkable Faith* will pick you back up and strengthen your heart for the journey God has called you to."

Lysa TerKeurst, *New York Times* bestselling author and president of Proverbs 31 Ministries

"Tracie Miles writes from personal experience and draws from the truths of Scripture as she shows you that unsinkable faith is a God-size transformation, setting you free to enjoy the positive, joyous, hope-filled life He designed for you!"

Liz Curtis Higgs, bestselling author of *Bad Girls of the Bible*

"Despite facing one of the most difficult situations a woman could face, Tracie realized she loved and trusted Jesus. Rather than succumbing to negativity, she submersed herself in the hope of God's Word. The result? An unsinkable faith penned into a book that will help other women keep their faith and their thoughts from sinking during hard times and make sure their faith strengthens along their journey."

Wendy Pope, speaker with Proverbs 31 Ministries and author of *Wait and See*

"For those of us looking to develop grit and resilience in this life, *Unsinkable Faith* is the guide we all need. Writing with hard-won wisdom, Tracie is the friend you want there with an outstretched hand to help you get on your feet again."

Kathi Lipp, bestselling author of
Overwhelmed and *The Husband Project*

"With powerful stories, poignant scripture, and practical steps to keep your faith buoyant in the storms of life, Tracie shows you not only how to survive the tsunamis of heartbreak but also how to thrive."

Sharon Jaynes, author of twenty-one books,
including *Take Hold of the Faith You Long
For* and *The Power of a Woman's Words*

"In *Unsinkable Faith*, Tracie vulnerably shares through her own story how we can break through the stronghold of negativity in our lives by fighting for control of our thoughts and emotions to live a more positive, victorious life!"

Michelle L. Bengtson, PhD, neuropsychologist
and author of *Hope Prevails*

"What if life suddenly hit you upside the head and sent your whole world reeling? How could you possibly maintain a deep faith and positive attitude in the midst of change and challenge? Author

Tracie Miles vulnerably shares how she has learned to do just that in her excellent new book, *Unsinkable Faith*."

Lucinda Secrest McDowell, author of *Dwelling Places* and codirector of reNEW (retreat for New England Writing), EncouragingWords.net

"*Unsinkable Faith* is a fantastic go-to guide for anyone who wants to revolutionize their thought life and transform the way they live. If you're feeling stuck in knowing how to begin the process and maintain positive thinking in such a negative world, this book is for you!"

Leah DiPascal, speaker and writer for Proverbs 31 First 5 app and *A Fresh Awakening*

"I expected a message of hope from *Unsinkable Faith*; what I didn't expect was to turn the last page feeling so boldly empowered. Tracie weaves carefully researched science with the incredible truth of God's Word and personal experiences to offer a life-altering message of encouragement to those who are feeling hurt, broken, or less than."

Courtney Westlake, author of *A Different Beautiful*

"How do we stand strong in the midst of life's negative thoughts and circumstances? In *Unsinkable Faith*, Tracie doesn't speak from theory; she speaks from her one hard and amazing life. She's real yet profound, tender yet challenging. If you feel like you're sinking yet yearning for hope, curl up with this friend of a book and you'll feel heard."

Courtney DeFeo, author of *In This House, We Will Giggle* and founder of Lil Light O' Mine

"Do you ever scroll through your social media feed and feel yourself sinking into a sea of negativity? I do. For those of us who struggle with negative thinking, Tracie has given us practical tools in *Unsinkable Faith* for beating it. And she reminds us that God can help."

Melanie Dale, author of *It's Not Fair* and *Women Are Scary*

"Tracie Miles is a woman I've watched be a positive influence in our generation. I often find myself struggling so much with thinking the right thoughts and believing the best is yet to come. Tracie's book is like a friend guiding me through the darkness of my murky thoughts toward the light God wants to pour in through Jesus."

Nicki Koziarz, author and speaker
with Proverbs 31 Ministries

"Tracie's new book has clued me in to paying attention not so much to the words I say but to the thoughts I think. I am already experiencing greater happiness by using her practical steps!"

Lynn Cowell, author of *Magnetic* and
speaker with Proverbs 31 Ministries

"Authentic and truth-filled, *Unsinkable Faith* is a relevant reminder of experiencing God's peace, even in the midst of less-than-perfect situations. As a woman who routinely struggles with 'stinkin' thinkin',' I see this resource as a go-to for many years to come."

Cindy Bultema, Bible teacher, speaker, and author
of *Live Full, Walk Free* and *Red Hot Faith*

UNSINKABLE

Faith

UNSINKABLE
Faith

God-Filled Strategies to Transform
the Way You Think, Feel, and Live

TRACIE MILES

DAVID C COOK

transforming lives together

UNSINKABLE FAITH
Published by David C Cook
4050 Lee Vance Drive
Colorado Springs, CO 80918 U.S.A.

Integrity Music Limited, a Division of David C Cook
Eastbourne, East Sussex BN23 6NT, England

The graphic circle C logo is a registered trademark of David C Cook.

The website addresses recommended throughout this book are offered as a
resource to you. These websites are not intended in any way to be or imply an
endorsement on the part of David C Cook, nor do we vouch for their content.

Details in some stories have been changed to protect
the identities of the persons involved.

Bible credits are listed at the back of the book.

LCCN 2016959766
ISBN 978-0-7814-1436-4
eISBN 978-1-4347-1026-0

The Author is represented by and this book is published in association with the
literary agency of WordServe Literary Group, Ltd., www.wordserveliterary.com.

The Team: Alice Crider, Liz Heaney, Nick Lee, Jack Campbell, Susan Murdock
Cover Design: Amy Konyndyk
Cover Photo: Getty Images

Printed in the United States of America
First Edition 2017

4 5 6 7 8 9 10 11 12 13

052318

Without these three people in my life, I wouldn't be who I am today. They help me stay positive, even when my thoughts try to pull me down, and they always give me a reason to smile. Morgan, Kaitlyn, and Michael—you are the lights of my life. To say I am thankful that God so immensely blessed me with the privilege of being your mom, and now the privilege of having you as my best friends, would be an understatement. I'm so proud of each of you and the amazing people you have grown into. I dedicate this book to you, not only because you stood by my side as my biggest supporters while it was being written, but because you are without a doubt the most beautiful, positive blessings I am eternally grateful for.

CONTENTS

PROLOGUE

Have you ever wondered what life might be like if you had a more optimistic attitude despite your past, present, or future circumstances? At a very young age, Margaret Tobin somehow decided that was exactly how she was going to live her life. Born in 1867, she endured a meager upbringing in a tiny, dirty two-room cottage on the banks of the Mississippi River in Missouri. "Maggie" was a scrappy, foul-mouthed tomboy who couldn't read or write but set her mind to becoming successful, refusing to let anything stand in her way.

At the age of eighteen, she moved to a small town in Colorado, and after years of perseverance, she eventually grew to be a popular American socialite, philanthropist, and activist for many great causes, such as women's rights and child literacy. She became well known for her many accomplishments. She was devout in her faith, which helped her attitude stay positive no matter how many hardships she faced, including the time she was on a ship that hit a large iceberg and began to sink.

When she realized what was happening, Maggie helped countless fellow passengers board the life rafts before she would get into one herself. Then later, wet and shivering in a life raft in the dark, cold sea in the middle of the night, and hearing the cries of those perishing off in the distance, she exhorted the crew on her raft to return to the capsizing vessel and look for additional survivors. She even took the oars into her own hands and helped row the raft back to the scene of the disaster. She encouraged the others in her boat not to give up hope, to work together, and to continue rowing until help was in sight.

Maggie not only survived the *Titanic* tragedy, she also helped others who had been rescued and even established a committee that raised nearly $10,000 for the survivors. She spent countless hours trying to contact families of passengers via telegraph, and she cared for survivors with food and blankets.

Her life was so inspiring, the press gave her a nickname of Molly, and soon a famous 1960 Broadway musical was created called *The Unsinkable Molly Brown*, which was also adapted into a movie in 1964 (Brown being her married name). The first scene of the movie sums up Molly's entire attitude. We see Molly's big brothers pestering her, yet again, and wrestling her to the ground, refusing to let her up until she hollered "Uncle." With all of their weight bearing down against her small frame, it was hard for her to break free, but that didn't stop her from fighting for victory. With dirt and feet flailing everywhere, their frenzied conversation in the midst of the brawl went like this:

> Brothers: "You're tuckered out, Molly! Why don't you quit?"

Molly (gasping for breath, with dirt in her mouth and eyes): "Sure I'm tuckered, and I might give out, but I won't give in! Nobody wants me down like I wants me up!"

Brothers continue to laugh and roughly wrestle her into the dirt, twisting her up like a pretzel.

Molly: "Now look-a-here, I am important to me! I ain't no bottom to no pile! I mean much more to me than anybody I ever knew! It doesn't make a bit of difference for you to keep telling me I'm down until I say so too! I hate that word, *down*, but I love the word *up* because that means hope; and that's just what I got. Hope."

Don't you just love that? Molly might have felt down or overcome, in fact physically she was both of those things. Yet mentally and emotionally, she refused to give in.

She was unsinkable.

How different would our lives look if we were as determined to have the unsinkable optimism and faith that Molly Brown had? What if we learned to start thinking more like her when we're faced with reasons to be negative or when we're feeling overpowered or beaten down by life, instead of always focusing on our problems and circumstances and letting them steal our peace, joy, and hope?

What if we refused to get *down* and put forth intentional effort into always being *up*, no matter what storms rage in our lives? How much more hopeful and joyful could we feel? How might our lives change if we acknowledge how important we are to Christ and start thinking of ourselves as people of utmost importance and value who don't deserve anything less than happy, joy-filled, peace-full lives? People who never belong on the bottom of a pile?

The real question is, how can we develop an unsinkable faith that carries us through life with a hopeful, positive attitude no matter what life throws at us?

Hop on board, my friend, because we are getting ready to take a journey to the land of optimism. If you've been sinking under the weight of negative thoughts, emotions, or circumstances for far too long, I have good news. There is a lighthouse off in the distance, gently waiting to lead you into calmer waters. And along the way, you're going to discover how to develop a positive mind, which leads to a more positive life, and how you too can have unsinkable faith.

Happiness is a state of mind.
It's just according to how you look at things.

Walt Disney

Chapter One

YOUR FEELINGS AREN'T THE BOSS OF YOU

When You Feel Like You're Sinking

When negative thoughts are controlling us, there is hope. When we learn to change the way we think, we can change the way we feel.

Life as I knew it had ended. And I had a choice to make. Either I could let my circumstances dictate my joy and happiness going forward, or I could intentionally choose to be positive and refuse to sink under the weight of negativity. That may have been the most important decision I've ever faced.

After nearly twenty-six years of marriage, my husband and I separated. The heartache and devastation were overwhelming, and I spent the first few months after he left in a puddle of tears and negative thoughts every day.

My vision of what the future was supposed to look like was wiped away in an instant, and my losses seemed to keep piling up. My fears about the uncertain future seemed innumerable, and I was consumed with worry for my children and how their parents' separation might affect their hearts. With each passing day, I felt the toxicity of negativity, hopelessness, fear, and pessimism seeping deeper and deeper into my heart. I felt as if I were stuck in a whirlpool, slowly being pulled under by the weight of my thoughts, yet desperately longing to be free and happy again. A tsunami had slammed into my reality, and as hard as I tried, I couldn't stop sinking into sadness and, at times, even felt I was struggling with depression.

But the day finally came, several months later, when my emotional and mental exhaustion seemed overwhelming, and I realized I was fed up with feeling sad and hopeless. I was tired of assuming the future couldn't be bright simply because the present was difficult. I knew that I needed to be a role model for my children and that my attitude would permeate theirs—either positively or negatively. I also knew that I needed to put my hope in God, trusting that not only was He able to heal broken hearts and broken relationships but also that, no matter what, I could have peace and joy if I intentionally invited Him to help me with my thoughts.

I realized I didn't want to spend my life being bitter and negative and stuck in pessimism, whether because of the current situation, hard circumstances that lay ahead, or simply the small struggles and frustrations of everyday life.

I certainly did not want to be the kind of person who always saw the glass half-empty instead of half-full and inadvertently overlooked her blessings because of the negative or bitter blinders on her heart. I had never been that type of person before, and in a moment with the One who holds all hope, I became determined I was never going to be.

My Conversation with Jesus That Changed Everything

I got on my knees and had a long conversation with Jesus, full of honest questions, anger, pleas, and tears. Then I sensed His voice whispering a gentle question to my spiritual ears, and my immediate answer caught me off guard. "Will you still love Me, Tracie?"

My answer, without hesitating, was "I still love You, Lord." I surprised myself with my response, but hearing my own heartfelt words brought comfort to my soul. Realizing I loved Jesus, despite what He had allowed in my life, gave me a renewed sense of hope. Not only in Him but also in myself. I knew it would not be easy, but I grabbed hold of the hope, peace, and reassurance He was offering and committed to holding on as tightly as I could.

As His peace washed over me, I knew that despite my circumstances and hardships, living a life of joy and positive thinking was within my reach, and that the first step of the journey had to be taken inside my own head. I had no control over my circumstances, but I could take control over my thoughts about them. I knew I needed to begin shifting my thoughts so that they didn't control my life.

My heart lightened when I surrendered my negativity and committed to trusting God through this storm. I realized optimism and positive thinking were still within my reach because I had the power within me through Christ to choose to be positive, despite my circumstances. I merely had to make an intentional effort to do so. And when I did, my whole perspective and outlook completely changed. My circumstances stayed the same, but over time, my thoughts and my heart did not.

Changing Our Perspectives, Regardless

I share this raw, personal pain with you only because I want you to know that I know what it's like to feel justified in living with a negative mind-set. I know what it's like to be upset with the situations God has either caused or allowed in our lives, and maybe even feel a little angry at Him. I know what it's like to desperately want situations to be different but to feel powerless to change them. And I know what it's like to long to be happy again and break free from the shackles of pain, heartache, and disappointment that pull down our spirits. But I also know what it's like to experience freedom from chronic negativity, and I want you to experience that too.

Today your situation and what pains your heart might be entirely different from what I've experienced. Or, maybe what I've described seems all too familiar. Friend, no matter what it is that might be draining your joy and robbing you of optimism, I know you must be struggling if you're reading a book to help you transform your mind so you can foster an unsinkable faith in your heart.

Maybe you want to be more positive but don't know how to change and are struggling to break free from the bondage of pessimism. Maybe you've convinced yourself you're doomed to be unhappy and negative because it seems your circumstances may never change and people have hurt you, physically or emotionally. Maybe you feel you don't deserve happiness because of mistakes you made in the past or because of patterns of sin or addictions in your life that you can't seem to break, making you feel like a failure time and time again. Or perhaps you've been battling depression and discouragement for so long, it seems impossible to ever overcome them. Maybe you feel as though you're drowning in a myriad of problems, barely able to keep your head above water in the storms of your life.

If any of these descriptions fit you, sweet friend, my heart goes out to you. I know those feelings all too well—been there, done that, and bought the T-shirt. More than once. But I've also learned that when our thoughts and attitudes get better, our lives can too, even if our circumstances remain the same. We can't always control how we feel, but we can always take authority over our own minds and change the way we think, which then changes the way we view and experience life overall.

When it feels like an overwhelming riptide of circumstances is causing us to sink, sometimes our faith and our attitudes are at risk of going down too. We feel like we just don't have the energy to keep fighting, and it becomes easier and easier to lose any hope that we'll ever make it safely to shore. But there is always hope—hope for a positive attitude, a stronger faith, a heart full of joy, and a happier future—when we put our hope in Jesus and choose not to let life cause us, or our attitudes, to sink. Even if we feel as though we're ready to give out, we don't have to give in to hopelessness and pessimism. If there is one thing for sure, it's that a negative mind will never lead you into a more positive life.

Regardless of where you find yourself today or how you're feeling, I want you to know that I get it. Not only because of my current trials but also because of many other difficulties I've experienced throughout my lifetime.

You Can Choose Life

We always have the power within us to choose how we think about our circumstances and our lives overall, despite what's going on. As believers we are all equipped to have hope when things seem hopeless, enabled to embrace joy when situations seem joyless, and empowered by the Holy Spirit within us to overcome the life-robbing habit of negative thinking.

We can learn to change our perspectives about our circumstances, even if our circumstances don't change. You see, when we learn to change the way we think, we can change the way we feel, which gradually transforms our minds to be more like Christ's, which then, in turn, changes the way we live, making our lives more positive. A changed mind will always result in a changed heart. A life of optimism and joy is possible for all of us, no matter what we're going through. After all, hearts anchored in God don't sink.

The encounter I had with Jesus when praying about my marriage was a game changer.

I am in no way saying making the choice to focus on the positive was easy—oh, friend, it was so not easy. Actually, it might have been the hardest thing I've ever had to do, especially in the midst of overwhelming heartache and disappointment. But deep in my spirit I knew that negativity could all too easily become a stronghold in my heart, my mind, and my life, and I also knew I could not let that happen.

Just because something bad had happened in my life didn't mean my life was bad, and just because I was unhappy in the moment didn't mean I had to live an unhappy life.

The Stronghold of Negativity

I didn't have to let negativity become a stronghold in my heart, and neither do you. I chose to try to be positive as much as possible and not to be held hostage to pessimism and bitterness. My prayer is that you will choose to do the same.

A stronghold is anything that holds us back from living life the way God intended and hinders our ability to live with optimism and full of peace, love, joy, and hope. When it comes to the term *stronghold*, people typically think of the obvious issues, such as sins, lying, stealing, worry, addictions, and so on. Yet all too often, it is our negative attitude that becomes a stronghold and keeps us from living a joy-filled life, not necessarily the external factors that influenced our attitude.

If a majority of our thoughts are negative, that "strong hold" of negativity can slowly choke out our happiness and keep us paralyzed in the land of pessimism, while we may live completely unaware this is happening. We may resort to blaming other people for the way we are feeling, struggling with fears, harboring anger, or assuming that God cannot love us or forgive us. We may assume He cares for everyone else, but not for us. We assume that no one else on the planet has ever gone through what we are going through and that nobody else could possibly relate.

We find ourselves not thinking Christlike thoughts, allowing fear and worry to run rampant in our hearts, letting the ups and downs of everyday life overwhelm us, or just mentally beating ourselves up for past mistakes or regrets. We might even justify our pessimism and negativity because we feel like a victim of others or of life. This hidden, inadvertent negativity can have a powerful impact on our lives. Our negative thoughts, if we ignore them, will dictate our feelings, and our feelings will dictate our actions. Thus, our unpleasant thoughts hold us hostage and have a "strong hold" on our outlook on life, our peace, and our joy.

Then one day we wake up and realize we are sinking in a pit of pessimism or anger or frustration, bitter about our circumstances, irritated at the smallest things, addicted to complaining and grumpiness, lacking peace and joy, snapping at our loved ones, and overall being discontent and unsatisfied with our lives and the people in it. If you ask me, the only thing worse than realizing we have become a full-blown pessimist is becoming one and never realizing it.

Fortunately, we each have the power within us as believers to fight this invisible battle for our thoughts. Second Corinthians

10:4 says, "We use our powerful God-tools for smashing warped philosophies, tearing down barriers erected against the truth of God, fitting every loose thought and emotion and impulse into the structure of life shaped by Christ" (THE MESSAGE). We have plenty of "God-tools" within our grasp to fight this spiritual war that takes place in our minds. We have God's Word, prayer, the prayers of others on our behalf, holy strength, perseverance, divine peace, and our faith walk, all of which equip us to push back against warped philosophies and our own minds' lies that do not line up with God's Word.

Although it's never easy to reshape our thoughts, especially when life feels hard, we can ask Christ to help us use those tools He has given us to chisel away at our negativity and lack of faith and to restructure our hearts, our minds, and ultimately our lives to be more like His. Satan's weapons don't stand a chance against God's power, but until we decide to pick up those God-tools, our spiritual weapons, and fight for control of our thoughts and emotions, he will continue to win the battle in our minds.

A Winnable Battle

We all know life can be hard. People hurt us, the past haunts us, coworkers mistreat us, parents don't love us, friends don't consider us, spouses don't honor us, children don't appreciate or respect us, finances don't support us, and our health doesn't sustain us. And when life gets hard, having a positive outlook and an optimistic attitude of joy can seem impossible to attain. But the apostle James tells us otherwise: "Dear brothers and sisters, when troubles of any kind come your way, consider it an opportunity for great joy" (1:2). We find this verse tucked within the story where the Christians of that time had allowed the frustrations and annoyances of life to steal their optimism and joy.

In their defense, these believers did have a lot of serious and justifiable reasons. They had been greatly persecuted, facing unrelenting trials and sufferings. They had experienced difficult adversities and injustices, from murder to imprisonment, at the hand of Saul, who was unrelentingly zealous in his efforts to destroy the church and anyone who associated with Christianity. As a result, these Christians were juggling an array of emotions, including fear, mourning, confusion, loneliness, and maybe even hopelessness. Some had fled their homes in fear of their lives, causing them to live in poverty and scrounge for every meal and penny. Some were sick, and everyone was exhausted. They had every right to be negative and pessimistic. James acknowledged their suffering, but he also let them know that inner joy and optimism could still be theirs, despite their adversities, if they deliberately chose to change their thinking. He encouraged them to pause and refocus on their faith, even when life was tough.

We may not experience religious persecution as the Jewish believers did, but let's face it: oftentimes life can make us feel persecuted. No matter what trying circumstance or difficult hardship we're enduring, we too are frequently faced with the choice of whether to let our circumstances steal our happiness. We too have to choose to fight against letting our troubles steal our joy and our ability to think positively. We too need to seek God's help in making those choices and carrying them out. Either we can think thoughts that are pitiful or we can think thoughts that are powerful. The choice is ours.

What might happen if we asked God to help us change our perspective about the current troubles we are facing? Although it might be difficult to endure our problems with a smile and an optimistic outlook, doing so with great faith results in more positive actions and helps us become stronger, more mature, more optimistic, and more joyful.

This was certainly true for my friend Lori. She shared with me the battle that went on in her mind for years, and how she used to live with overwhelming fear.

As a little girl, she was afraid of her babysitters, teachers, meeting new friends, and speaking up in class. As she grew up, her fears morphed into a paralyzing stronghold that affected her entire life. She feared meeting new people, of living with roommates in college, and even of dating. Eventually, Lori's fears caused her to retreat into her own shell, becoming very shy and withdrawn in an attempt to feel safe, and at times being afraid to leave her home at all.

Just before her college graduation, she was raped, and all the accompanying shame, guilt, anxiety, and newly heightened fear began to hold her hostage in her own body. She was a prisoner to the thoughts in her head, and they had a strong hold on her life as a whole. Her negative thoughts influenced her feelings, which affected her life, which negatively affected her happiness.

But thankfully, Lori eventually grew tired of being imprisoned by fear, and one day she made the hard, yet life-changing choice to do something about it. She reached up to God and asked Him to help her change her thought patterns and take control of her life.

She began doing Bible studies to help her become more confident in who she was and to learn to understand the spiritual weapons at her disposal as a child of God. She began to recognize the mental and emotional prison her strongholds were keeping her in and gradually learned how to break free from them by reading and memorizing God's Word and spending time in prayer and journaling. She surrendered her fears to God and refused to live a lonely life full of worries and negative thinking. One little step of faith at a time, she overcame the stronghold of fear in her mind and embraced a life with less fear and more joy. Her decision to take control of her thoughts equipped her to take control of her life and her happiness.

In a similar way, shortly after I had my "I still love You, Lord" conversation with Jesus, I knew I needed to retake control of my thoughts. I realized I had been struggling with many negative mental strongholds, one of which was fear. Each morning I would wake up and the suffocating fears of what the present day, and the future, might hold would creep into my consciousness. I had become consumed with all the what-ifs. Nine times out of ten my what-ifs were followed up with a worst-case-scenario theory that pulled me deeper into darkness and hopelessness.

So I committed to working on my attitude and to surrendering all the fears that had been building up in my head for months.

I got out my journal and wrote down my fears one by one and, within minutes, had written out thirty-three fears. Thirty. Three. Paralyzing. Fears. Have mercy.

I didn't realize until that moment how my fears had multiplied or how much they were damaging my attitude, much less that they had such a strong power over my thoughts and perspectives. Immediately, I surrendered those fears and all the accompanying emotions to God in prayer and since have taken a stand to keep them from slipping back into my subconscious.

The difference that prayer of surrender made in my outlook and my life going forward amazed even me. Although my emotions and feelings were valid and justified, I had allowed them to take over my mind and, in turn, take over my life and my happiness, and this little journaling activity was an eye opener.

Don't Give Up!

Maybe today your circumstances have caused you to struggle with overwhelming fears or strong emotions that make you feel like you're sinking in negativity or drowning in pessimism. If so, please don't beat yourself up—and for goodness sake, please don't give up on yourself! God created us to be emotional creatures, and whatever feelings we have are legitimate and valid. In fact, our emotions are like indicator lights on a car's dashboard: they point to something that needs attention, and in this case, it's our thoughts. Emotions are fueled by our thoughts, and that's okay, but Jesus never wanted us to be held hostage by them. He knew life would be hard and reassures us all throughout the Bible of His presence, even when we are feeling persecuted by life or people. As we lean into Him and confess our desire to be transformed inside and out, the impossible becomes possible. For you and for me and for all of God's beloveds.

Proverbs 23:7 says, "For as he thinks in his heart, so is he" (NLV). In other words, what we think will be evident in our outward attitudes and actions. This means that our thoughts are nothing to take for granted. Our perspectives and thoughts hold the power to determine our attitudes and also our tomorrows. Fortunately, we get to choose what our tomorrows look like, one thought and one day at a time. In the words of Norman Vincent Peale, a popular minister and author, "Change your thoughts and you change your world."[1]

True joy and a positive attitude come from the choice to change your thoughts, not from a problem-free life. So, sweet friend, let today be the first day of your new optimistic life. Let it be the first day of a fresh season of life when you begin living a life of optimism, seeing the glass as half-full, instead of half-empty.

You are not alone in this battle. We can either give up or God-up, and when we God-up, He always shows up. As we sojourn through this book, we'll be unpacking three God-filled strategies that we need to put into practice in our daily lives if we want to transform our thoughts, feelings, and lifestyles:

1. *Notice* negative thoughts.
2. *Reject* negative thoughts.
3. *Replace* negative thoughts.

Scripture reinforces the importance of these three steps: "We demolish arguments and every pretension that sets itself up against the knowledge of God, and we take captive every thought to make it obedient to Christ" (2 Cor. 10:5 NIV). If you're like me, you've always known this instruction was important but never really understood how to follow through. How do we take our thoughts captive and then change our lives? Well, sister, we'll be exploring just that as we move forward in this journey toward optimism and joy.

As you read, I pray that God will open the door of your heart and help you begin to let your faith be in control of your mind so you can take back your thoughts. If you are ready to be rescued, God is ready to pull you out of the muck of negativity and discouragement. My hope is that when you get to the last page of this book, you will find yourself on the shores of a breathtaking place you didn't know existed—a beautiful land where a positive mind and an optimistic heart thrive.

STRATEGIES FOR TRANSFORMING YOUR THINKING

At the end of each chapter, you'll find several questions to help you apply to your own situation what you're learning from Tracie. These will help you get unstuck! So grab a journal or notebook from your closet, or purchase the accompanying journal from Tracie's website, www.traciemiles.com, and commit to this work that will help you find freedom.

- This book is in your hands for a reason. What situation in your life today triggers the most dissatisfaction or distress? There may be several, but start with just one. Hold it in your heart as you read the rest of this book. Name it in your journal and write a prayer offering the person or situation to God. Close your eyes and picture God's gracious hands receiving your burden and gently holding this concern for you. Throughout the rest of this book, keep that image in your heart and mind.
- It would have been easy for Tracie to blame someone else for her distressing feelings. Make a comprehensive list of others you have blamed for your own circumstances. While some may *deserve* that blame, focusing on blame will only keep you stuck. Pray through each person, releasing him or her to God. Imagine the chain of blame being attached to an anchor pulling you down, and when you let go of those thoughts, picture yourself being released from captivity.

- There was a moment when Tracie realized she didn't want to spend her life stuck in negativity and unhappiness. Can you think of particular conversations, interactions, or private moments when you knew that something needed to change? Did someone else notice your negativity, or did you? Record those encounters—with others, with God, or with yourself—that made you want to live differently.

- What could be different in your life if you committed yourself to this process? Describe how you would be different, inside and out.

Mind-Renewing Memory Verses

A key strategy for transforming our minds involves replacing lies and negative thoughts with promises and truths from God's Word that refute those lies and fill our minds with hope instead. Below are some verses that you can copy in your journal, notepad, or on notecards so you can read them throughout the week. Committing these verses to memory will build a spiritual arsenal that you can call on when negativity strikes and is an important step in winning the war for your thoughts.

> The weapons we fight with are not the weapons
> of the world. On the contrary, they have divine
> power to demolish strongholds. (2 Cor. 10:4 NIV)

Consider it pure joy, my brothers and sisters, whenever you face trials of many kinds, because you know that the testing of your faith produces perseverance. Let perseverance finish its work so that you may be mature and complete, not lacking anything. If any of you lacks wisdom, you should ask God, who gives generously to all without finding fault, and it will be given to you. (James 1:2–5 NIV)

You, LORD, give true peace
> to those who depend on you,
> > because they trust you. (Isa. 26:3 NCV)

We demolish arguments and every pretension that sets itself up against the knowledge of God, and we take captive every thought to make it obedient to Christ. (2 Cor. 10:5 NIV)

For as he thinks in his heart, so is he. (Prov. 23:7 NLV)

Chapter Challenge

In your journal, or even using a notes or memo app on your phone, begin keeping track of each time you find yourself struggling with a negative thought or emotion. Don't judge yourself for them. Just notice and record them. Then, each time you record something, ask God to intervene and begin equipping you spiritually to think and feel differently. Tracie will let you know what to do with them soon! For now, simply offer these to God.

*The quality of your life depends
on the quality of your thoughts.*

A. R. Bernard

Chapter Two

TENS OF THOUSANDS OF REASONS

Why We Sink

We sink because of how we think!
Thoughts, and not circumstances, determine
whether we're anchored in negativity.

An obviously grumpy old man, wearing a scowl on his face, walked into a restaurant and confronted the hostess, unsure if he wanted to eat at that particular establishment. She looked up at his glare and hesitantly asked, "Can I help you, sir?"

The cranky man huffed under his breath and quickly blurted out his question: "Do you serve crabs here?"

And the waitress smirked wryly and said, "Why, yes, sir. We serve anybody here."

This joke gave me a chuckle when I heard it, but it made me wonder how many times I'd walked around looking and feeling crabby without even realizing it, all because of negative thoughts swirling in my mind.

A few years ago I ran into the grocery store to pick up a few items for dinner and must have looked similar to this crabby old man. I was standing there, minding my own business and waiting to pay my bill, when the clerk abruptly stopped ringing up my items, looked me straight in the eye, and loudly bellowed, "Smile, ma'am. It can't be all that bad!"

His comment snapped me back into reality and caught me completely off guard. It wasn't until that moment that I realized my facial expression had clearly implied I was in a sour mood. I didn't mean to look rude, unhappy, or pessimistic, but my inward thoughts, which were mentally stewing over the day's problems, were affecting how I felt, which was reflected in my facial expression and demeanor, which in turn affected my outward behavior more than I realized. I was apparently looking like a big ol' pessimistic crab, yet I was blind to how my thoughts were affecting me—inside and out—and how they were affecting those around me.

When life isn't going as we would like, when people have hurt us, or when our problems seem overwhelming or hopeless, it's tempting to choose negativity. We can easily become blinded to the vibe we are giving off or to how our thoughts are affecting our lives overall, especially if our negativity has become so commonplace that it's not only a stronghold in our hearts but also a subconscious, daily habit that other people can see.

Negative Thoughts→Negative Feelings→Negative Life

The average person has 50,000 to 70,000 thoughts per day, which equates to 35 to 48 thoughts per minute.[1] Approximately 95 percent of our thoughts today are the same thoughts we thought yesterday.[2] To make matter worse, about 80 percent of those habitual thoughts are negative ones. Tens of thousands of negative thoughts cycle through our minds day after day after day, poisoning our attitudes and our outlooks, one by one.[3]

Eighty percent of tens of thousands of little thoughts add up to a lot of negative thinking and self-talk. If the majority of our thoughts are positive, then we'll feel and be more positive, but if the majority of our self-talk is negative? Well, let's just say the outcome will not be pretty. You see, it is our thoughts that drive our feelings and our happiness, not our circumstances. If our thoughts are negative, our feelings and actions will be negative as well, and altogether those things can lead to a negative life, lacking peace and joy.

For example, if we spend an entire day fuming over our spouse's flaws and thinking about how he doesn't meet our needs, we will *feel* animosity toward him or, at minimum, a lack of love, which leads to outward negative behaviors that might damage the relationship.

If we spend time thinking about how our boss doesn't appreciate us and constantly telling ourselves how underpaid we are, we will *feel* discontent at our job, which can lead to a bad attitude, poor performance, or maybe the unemployment line.

If we spend time thinking about what other people think about us, we will *feel* like we don't measure up and live with a lack of confidence in who we are, and Whose we are.

If we constantly think about our past mistakes rather than accept God's forgiveness and mercy, we will *feel* unforgivable and unlovable and live a life disconnected from the love and acceptance He wants us to embrace.

If we let the critical words a parent said to us when we were children, the rejection or hurtful actions of a spouse, or the judgment of a friend or loved one dwell in our thoughts and define how we think about ourselves, we will *feel* like worthless individuals incapable of living life with purpose.

If we listen to all this negative self-talk, which is not from God, we might end up sinking in an ocean of discouragement and hopelessness and *feeling* that we can never swim our way out to peaceful waters.

You see, our thoughts turn into feelings that can easily take control of our lives and steer us in a direction we do not want to go. Our feelings are persistent and unrelenting, constantly whispering to gain dominion over our actions. They can create our destiny, either good or bad, because whatever we are dwelling on in our minds is what will play out in our lives. It is usually our thoughts, not our circumstances, that cause us to sink. This is such an important truth to tuck into our minds. Mark it down: what we think becomes who we are.

I know this to be true because I've experienced it. Because of one very unfortunate decision I made as a teenager, I lived for years under the weight of negative, self-condemning thoughts. All those negative thoughts in my mind had shaped my view of myself and influenced my actions in a destructive way.

Shortly after my first year of college, I went to an abortion clinic. The people at the clinic told me they could help me take care of "the problem" and I'd never have to think about it again. I had already filled my mind with self-condemning thoughts, and those thoughts coupled with fear and shame caused me to believe their lies and to put my trust and hope in them instead of in God. And while I'd been promised that I would never have to think about "the problem" again, that wasn't what happened. I thought about my mistake every single day for many, many years.

Each day I habitually reminded myself of my secret, mentally beating myself up, constantly listening to the lie that God could never forgive me and convincing myself that I didn't deserve His forgiveness anyway. Daily negative thoughts flooded my mind until the self-condemnation spilled over, pulling me down further and further into the murky darkness of shame and regret.

Because I was constantly dwelling on my sin, I *felt* I didn't deserve to be happy. I *felt* I didn't deserve to be at peace. I *felt* unworthy to be a daughter of God. I *felt* my life would always be scarred by my past and God could not possibly have a plan and purpose for my life. I *felt* I deserved whatever sufferings or hardships I faced.

I believed God was a forgiving heavenly Father and a loving God—for everyone but me. My thoughts told me that my sin was just too horrific for even God to forgive, and I *felt* like I should never forgive myself either.

For over a decade, I wore a smile on my face, while my tear-stained heart sank deeper and deeper in regret and shame, all because of what my mind was dwelling on—lies from the enemy that I had come to believe were truths. Consequently, I was disconnected from God and deeply discouraged. My thoughts, fueled by the enemy who wanted to keep me down, drove my feelings about myself, which fueled how I lived my life and negatively affected my inner peace and overall happiness. I had erected a mental barrier between God and me, all because I *thought* I didn't deserve His mercy and didn't feel worthy of His grace and love.

Here's the thing: God wasn't telling me I should be ashamed; I told myself that. God didn't say He didn't love me and couldn't forgive me; I told myself that. God didn't say I deserved to be unhappy and endure difficult circumstances; I told myself that. God didn't say He was going to punish me for my sin; I came up with that belief in my own mind. God didn't say I couldn't ever have inner peace and optimism; I thought that on my own.

But then one day at a women's seminar at my church, as I sat in a sea of worshipping women, all that changed. I heard God's voice reverberate in my spirit loud and clear, and I invited Him into those dark places. Sitting quietly in the church pew, I bowed my head, tears dropping onto my lap, and asked God for forgiveness, again, for probably the millionth time over a fourteen-year span. But in that divine moment, my heart was desperately seeking Him. My spiritual eyes and ears were opened and I finally accepted and believed once and for all that I was truly forgiven and loved.

Yes, I had messed up, but that didn't mean I was an irreparable mess to God. He wasn't keeping a record of my wrongs ("[Love] … keeps no record of wrongs"—1 Cor. 13:5 NIV), and I no longer needed to either. He had forgiven me when I had asked Him to years ago; however, over time, my thoughts and feelings had convinced me otherwise. But in that divine encounter, I felt His love, acceptance, and peace surging through my soul.

For the first time in my life, I had experienced what it felt like to be cleansed and washed white as snow, just as we are told is possible in Isaiah 1:18: "'Come now, let's settle this,' says the LORD. 'Though your sins are like scarlet, I will make them as white as snow. Though they are red like crimson, I will make them as white as wool.'" On that day, the Lord settled it and I accepted it. I vowed to let the past be the past and to never pick up that particular burden of shame again. I asked God to transform my mind and chose to give Him, instead of the enemy of my soul, dominion over my thoughts and feelings.

When God replaced the shame that swirled inside my mind with the truth of His radical love and forgiveness and I began to *think* differently, I *felt* differently too, like a whole new person! Had I not sought God's intervention to transform my heart and mind on that memorable day, picked up the spiritual weapon of faith and intentionally chosen to fight for control of my thoughts, I have no doubt my life would look entirely different today. It's certainly not perfect, and not without troubles, but my faith is unsinkable and so is my God. That experience helped me discover that I have the power within me to live a positive life, no matter what. I began building a foundation in my heart and mind for hopeful, optimistic thinking and learned the importance of controlling my thoughts, whether they are about my past, what I'm facing today, or what is to come. And so can you.

You Don't Have to Sink

We're all going to face difficult circumstances and storms, and problems are inevitable, but we don't have to let our thoughts about those circumstances and problems sink us. It's all a matter of what we choose to think about and fill our heads with.

Ships, whether huge barges or tiny sailboats, don't sink because they get caught in a storm or because of the towering waves tossing them about. They sink because of the water that gets inside of their hulls. We may have no control over the storms in our lives, the mistakes of our past, or the circumstances around us, but we do have control over what we choose to think about and what we tell ourselves. We don't have to let the storms of life get inside of us and cause us to sink because we have the power in Christ to guard our hearts, if only we seek it out. When our hearts are guarded, our thoughts and feelings are too, and we will be more likely to stay above the stormy waters instead of being tossed about or even pulled under by a current of negativity.

While it is impossible to control *all* of the thousands of thoughts that enter our minds every day, we can learn to notice them and become aware of them, especially those thoughts that are not positive or grounded in God's truths. I wonder if the reason many of us don't ask God for mind transformation is that we don't realize we are stuck in negative thought patterns. Or perhaps we know we are stuck in negativity or a victim mentality, but we feel justified in feeling the way we do. The truth of the matter is this: we can ask God for nothing more important, other than salvation and eternal life, than for Him to transform and renew our hearts and minds.

Starting the Transformation

Attitude transformations don't happen overnight, but they do happen. You have the power in Christ to stop letting your thoughts and feelings cause you to sink; you can grab hold of the hope and joy He is offering. You can have hope for a renewed mind and an amazing life, despite your past, present, or future mess-ups and problems, and despite how long you've had a negative mind-set. You can have hope for an unshakable peace, even when storms seem to be raging all around you, threatening to pull you under. You can learn to think positively and to have hope, even when life feels out of control. You can live happily and full of joy, even if all of the adversity in your life seems to justify your being unhappy, and even if you've been feeling like a grumpy ol' crab for way too long.

All believers have the power of the Holy Spirit within them to break down the stronghold of negativity in their lives, no matter how many years negative thinking has taken up residence in their minds. Believers can learn to submit their thoughts to God if they choose to put in the effort and practice the daily renewing of their minds, as we are told to do in Romans 12:2: "Don't copy the behavior and customs of this world, but let God transform you into a new person by changing the way you think. Then you will learn to know God's will for you, which is good and pleasing and perfect." This verse holds the fundamental principle for positive thinking and joyful living. If we conform to the world, instead of to God, we are headed straight toward a life lacking peace, joy, and hope. But when we let Christ renew our minds, we will be blessed with the ability to enjoy life, despite life.

Trust me, I realize this is easier said than done. However, I'm confident we can all find victory over our thoughts, with God's help.

It would be nice if God would simply control our thoughts for us, but instead He has given us free will. Our free will influences our thinking, which fuels our attitude and state of mind. For that reason we are told, "Guard your heart above all else, for it determines the course of your life" (Prov. 4:23). When the author of this proverb refers to guarding our hearts, he is talking about the inner core of who we are. Our inner core is our feelings, desires, choices, actions, moods, and so on—all of which are driven by our thoughts. Our thoughts make up not only who we are but also who we will become and where we will end up, because our inward thoughts usually dictate our outward actions.

Even though God doesn't automatically take charge of our thoughts, as soon as we are ready for His intervention, He will help us learn to guard our hearts so that bitterness and negativity stay out of the place where He resides. You're free to be you and I'm free to be me, according to God's divine plan. But why not be the best we can be by asking Him to help us control our thoughts so that we can enjoy the inner peace and joy He offers us?

If something bad happens to us, we don't have to start believing we have a bad life. When we experience something positive in the morning but have to deal with something negative in the afternoon, we have the choice to say whether we've had a good day or a bad day overall. If someone insults us or hurts our feelings, we can forgive and refuse to let it fester in our thoughts and steal our confidence, and we can focus our positive attributes and remember it is what God thinks that is most important. Each time our minds wander to a place where discouragement, sadness, fear, anger, or negativity reside, and we notice our feelings are changing our moods, perspectives, and behavior, we have the authority to take those thoughts captive and shift our thoughts to be more positive.

Our thoughts have power over our lives, because it's our minds that choose to focus on good or bad and whether to believe the enemy's lies. It's with our minds that we choose whether to follow God's instructions for thinking and living. When we admit our need for change, and ask God to start the process of thought transformation in us, He does so. My friend Kimberly will attest to that.

Kimberly's Journey

Kimberly and her husband tried and tried to conceive a child, but Kimberly just couldn't get pregnant. They even went to a fertility specialist, but after months and months and many unsuccessful treatments, her doctors told her she would never be able to get pregnant. Kimberly was open to adoption, but her husband was not. He wanted his own biological children, and eventually the marriage ended.

Not only did Kimberly feel as though she were somehow less of a woman because she could not bear a child, but the divorce left her feeling rejected and discarded. In the months and years following, she formed a mental habit of continually telling herself she was worthless. She felt bitter, lonely, and sad. The future looked bleak … hopeless. Kimberly struggled for years to push through the pain and unforgiveness, but her thoughts held her captive to negativity and wreaked havoc on her self-esteem and confidence.

But as she continued to walk in faith, she invited God to help her transform her mind and renew her thoughts on a daily basis, and He did exactly that. Over time, He opened her eyes to see that He was giving her opportunities to work with children. He showed her that she played a vital role in helping rear her nieces and nephews. She realized that although she couldn't bear children of her own, she could still pour into the lives of little ones in many different ways.

As God transformed her thoughts, Kimberly began to believe that neither her infertility nor the rejection of her ex-husband defined her value as a person, a woman, or a treasured child of God. She became determined to think positively about herself and her future. She asked God to help her forgive those who had hurt her, and she began reading His Word, leaning on her faith, and seeking after God with all her heart to find the healing and acceptance she longed for.

Kimberly intentionally chose to change her thought life from negative to positive, and as a result, she experienced God's peace, joy, and blessings. Her changed thoughts changed her feelings, which changed her life in a brand-new, positive way. Eventually she married a godly man who loves her unconditionally. He loves her for who she is, not what she can give him. But please take note of this important fact: Kimberly's life didn't change because her relationship status changed. It changed because her thoughts changed. Toxic thinking will always stand in the way of God's greatest blessings. In order for Kimberly's life to be transformed, her heart and mind had to undergo a radical transformation first.

Change Is Possible

You see, life just happens, but positive thinking doesn't. Our thoughts, not our circumstances, determine the condition of our hearts and minds. Our thoughts elicit our feelings, so if we change our thoughts, we can change how we feel. I know we can't always just talk ourselves into feeling differently, but we can learn to be more aware of how our thoughts are making us feel, ask for God's help, and practice control over our thoughts. When we intentionally ask God to lead us through a radical mind transformation and choose to be positive despite negative circumstances and feelings, our thoughts, feelings, and lives as a whole change for the better. In my experience it doesn't work to just "try harder" to control our thoughts and feelings, especially when our circumstances or hardships are staying the same. But when we seek God's help in transforming our minds, we put ourselves back into a position of power—a position to reclaim power over our thoughts and over our lives.

You don't have to be sitting in a sea of worshipping women to experience the same freedom from negativity that I did all those years ago. In fact, you can experience it right now, because wherever you are sitting and reading this book, Jesus is right beside you with open arms and love and compassion in His eyes. He knows there are many hard circumstances you've lived through that have legitimately caused you to struggle with negativity and pessimism. Maybe you've even doubted God's ways or His goodness. Or even His love. He knows that too. He knows whatever it is that has stolen your joy, your self-confidence, and/or your ability to be positive—whether it be current difficult circumstances, seasons of pain, or hurtful people. He knows you're only human and understands all of that, and instead of condemnation, His thoughts toward you remain loving and positive.

We read in Psalm 139:17–18, "How precious are your thoughts about me, O God. They cannot be numbered! I can't even count them; they outnumber the grains of sand! And when I wake up, you are still with me!" I don't know about you, but hearing that beautiful promise pours fresh joy into my heart. No matter how deep our pessimism goes, the reasons for it, or how long we've struggled, God's countless thoughts toward us are nothing but sweet and precious. He is always with us wherever we go.

I pray you will stick with me as we continue to look at how you can change the way you think, feel, and live. The next chapter will help you understand why taking our thoughts captive is so crucial, and how to start forming a habit of doing just that. Even if you can't see the shore yet, hold on tight to the hope God is offering and believe that a mind makeover is possible. Visualize a fresh season of life on the horizon, one where you intentionally choose to live a life of optimism and joy, arising each morning with a peaceful heart, a positive outlook, and a smile on your face, despite the troubles or challenges the day may hold.

Such is the life of a positive thinker, and with commitment and dedication, it is a life that is possible for all of us in Christ— including you.

STRATEGIES FOR TRANSFORMING YOUR THINKING

Mind-Transforming Reflections

- Tracie noted that the average person has 50,000 to 70,000 thoughts per day. As you begin to pay attention to your thoughts—noting in your journal or on your phone—what are some of the thoughts that get more "air time" than the rest? Write down the top three to five negative thoughts that you notice most often.

- Tracie bravely shared the way her decision to have an abortion caused her to get stuck in a place of negativity in her heart and mind. Though she believed in God's grace for others, she struggled to receive it for herself. That single decision, for which God had forgiven her, triggered thoughts, for *years*, that kept her stuck in shame and guilt, preventing her from loving herself and from believing God had a plan and purpose for her life. Write down any circumstances from the past—ones for which you were responsible and ones for which you were not responsible—that have trapped you in a mind-set of negativity and become a stronghold in your thinking. Then offer these to God.

- Kimberly is a great example of a woman whose thinking changed before her circumstances did. Name the circumstances in your life that seem unlikely to change. Offer those to God with the confidence that they need not sink you.

- Tracie reminded you that Jesus is with you right now. Close your eyes and notice His gracious face. Drink in the compassion and love Jesus is offering you in this moment. Enjoy Jesus's presence, knowing that He receives you exactly as you are.

Mind-Renewing Memory Verses

Write out the verses below in your journal, or on your notecards, and try to commit them to memory.

> Come, let's talk this over, says the Lord; no matter how deep the stain of your sins, I can take it out and make you as clean as freshly fallen snow. Even if you are stained as red as crimson, I can make you white as wool! (Isa. 1:18 TLB)

> For you created my inmost being;
>> you knit me together in my mother's womb.
> I praise you because I am fearfully and
>> wonderfully made;
>> your works are wonderful,
>> I know that full well. (Ps. 139:13–14 NIV)

How precious are your thoughts about me,
    O God.
        They cannot be numbered!
I can't even count them;
        they outnumber the grains of sand!
And when I wake up,
        you are still with me! (Ps. 139:17–18)

Don't copy the behavior and customs of this world, but let God transform you into a new person by changing the way you think. (Rom. 12:2)

Guard your heart above all else,
        for it determines the course of your life.
            (Prov. 4:23)

Chapter Challenge

It's our thinking, and not our circumstances, that determines how we feel. Though it might take a while to sink in, that is really good news! Make a list of all the circumstances in your life that need not determine how you feel. Start by noting the circumstances you're facing today—at home, at work, at church, in your marriage, in your extended family, and/or in your community. Also include circumstances from the past that continue to swirl in your heart and mind. When you're done, read that list of circumstances and announce, "You, circumstances, do not determine my satisfaction or happiness!"

Which of the verses from this chapter speak most to your heart about this life-transforming reality that your circumstances need not win? How does it encourage you today?

Proverbs 4:23
1 Corinthians 13:5
Isaiah 1:18
Romans 12:2
Psalm 139:17–18

Or jot down another passage of Scripture that strengthens you to reject the lie that your circumstances determine your happiness. Choose one verse to hold in your heart and mind this week. Tape it to your nightstand or bathroom mirror so you can speak it aloud when you awake and before you sleep.

Change your thoughts and you change your world.

Norman Vincent Peale

Chapter Three

COUNT THE COST

What We Lose When We Go Down

Because negative thinking puts our hearts, minds, health,
and relationships at risk, pause and count the cost.

She was ninety-two years old, petite and poised, sporting perfect makeup and cute outfits every day of the week. Her husband of seventy years had recently passed away, and she now had no other choice but to move out of the home she'd always known and into a nursing home. On the day of the move, after patiently waiting in the lobby of the nursing home for quite some time, a smile washed across her face when a staff member told her that her room was finally ready. As the elderly woman carefully maneuvered her walker to the elevator and shuffled her feet behind it, the nurse explained to the woman what her room looked like. She described the dainty eyelet curtains on the window, the fresh white sheets on the bed, and the flower vase on her nightstand with yellow sunflowers in it.

She started to say more, but the woman interrupted her and enthusiastically exclaimed, "Oh, I love it!" The nurse chuckled and reminded her she hadn't even seen the room yet. To which the woman quickly responded with a profound statement that took the nurse by surprise.

The elderly woman leaned in close and said, "I don't have to see it, honey, because happiness is something you decide on ahead of time. Whether I like my room or not doesn't depend on what it looks like, what the window view is, how it smells, or if I like the curtains. You see, I have already decided to love it and be happy in it. No matter what."

The nurse stood there, mouth gaping.

The old woman continued, "Happiness is a decision I make each morning when I wake up. I have a choice. I can spend the day in bed thinking about how my body doesn't work anymore like it used to, or I can be thankful I'm still alive. I can focus on the difficult times I've been through, and the loss of those I loved, or I can choose to be happy for what today will bring and find joy in God and the people who surround me. Each day is a gift, and as long as my eyes open, I can choose to focus on the new day and all the happy memories I've tucked into my heart, just for this specific time in my life."

Versions of this sweet story have been circulating the Internet for years, and regardless if it is factual, the point it makes is certainly true. This woman had discovered that in order for her to be positive and optimistic and have a happy outlook on life, she had to choose not to let seeds of negativity and bitterness plant themselves into her thoughts. She had to focus on the good things God had placed in her life, even in the littlest of blessings, instead of the not-so-good things. She purposely made a daily, conscious choice to be positive, no matter what.

In her ninety-two years of living, she'd discovered happiness and peace were within her control and did not hinge on the circumstances around her. She practiced and mastered the skill of choosing mind over emotions. As a result, she was able to feel joyful even when life got difficult. That is what we all have the power to do if we so choose, and that choice changes our destiny.

When we allow life's circumstances or other people to hold the key to our joy, we will always risk losing it. Instead of living acutely aware of the blessings God bestows on us each day, we may instead go through life feeling unhappy, sad, disappointed, or dissatisfied with how life has turned out.

Let's take a closer look at the price we pay when we succumb to negativity and pessimism.

The Cost to Our Relationships

Negativity is costly and carries the threat of destroying family, relationships, friendships, work environments, and even churches. When we're held hostage by negativity, we wonder why everyone else has it easier than us. It can cause us to miss out on being a blessing to others because we are so focused on ourselves and our long list of issues. We may even inadvertently become such a negative person that other people avoid us.

My friend Renee told me that this was exactly what happened in her life. Renee was diagnosed with rheumatoid arthritis twelve years ago when she was forty-one years old. The disease gradually progressed to the point where she was no longer able to dress or feed herself. She became angry and negative, even mad at God. Once in a heated moment of prayer, she yelled at God and told Him she wasn't happy with what He had allowed in her life. It wasn't fair. Through her tears and anger, she felt a gentle whisper brush through her mind, "Do you want people around you, or do you want to be all alone?" While the question caught her off guard, Renee knew in her heart it came from God. She wiped her tears and began to ponder what God might be saying to her. She soon recognized that if her thoughts remained angry, negative, and grumpy, and if she was always complaining and whining and acting ill tempered and unhappy, eventually no one would want to be around her—even if her feelings were justified.

While Renee didn't want her negativity to isolate her friends and family, she realized that it was indeed affecting her relationships and actually driving some people away. If she continued to be bitter, she may one day be bitter all alone. She knew how much she needed and wanted support and loving friends in her life, so she began to pray for God to transform her mind and equip her with an attitude of optimism. She chose to take control of her thoughts instead of letting them control her attitude.

Her attitude didn't change immediately, but as she walked in faith and intentionally tried to change her thinking habits, she slowly began to shift her outlook and her attitude. Now, although her circumstances have remained the same, she is blessed with several precious friends who come and stay with her on a daily basis—not because they have to, but because they want to. Had Renee chosen to hold on to negativity, it's likely that her daily routines, the people in her life, the blessings she enjoys, and her overall happiness would look much different.

Another friend told me how the constant negativity of her in-laws eventually prevented her and her family from visiting them as often. My friend realized how easy it was to get caught up in negativity and noticed how it was affecting her and her children. Her in-laws' negativity drove away the people they loved, and they may not have even realized the damage they were causing.

Another woman confided that her mother was so habitually critical of her and her sister when they were young that it made their home a toxic place to live. Their mother was always speaking negatively about them to others and berating them constantly. She and her sister both got married at a young age and moved out of state in order to escape the negativity. They didn't want themselves or their families to be exposed to it any more than necessary, not just because it was so wounding, but also because they knew it could spread.

The Cost to Our Hearts

God knows the havoc negativity and pessimism can wreak in our lives, and I believe that is why there are so many beautiful scriptures about being aware of what we put into our hearts and minds. God knows long-term negativity eventually leads to bitterness, which can not only consume our minds but also harden our hearts and change who we are. That is exactly what happened to Naomi in the book of Ruth.

Naomi was married to Elimelech, who was a very wealthy man because of the rich agricultural area they lived in, in Israel. Naomi had everything she could possibly want. Life was full; in fact, her name actually meant "pleasantness."[1] But in the beginning of the book of Ruth, we learn Naomi lived during a very difficult time. It was considered the time of judges, which according to Scripture, was a time of chaos.

Judges 17:6 says, "In those days Israel had no king; all the people did whatever seemed right in their own eyes." "Those days" describes four hundred years of dark days and oppression. Because God's people did not follow His law and worshipped idols, God sent a famine across the land, and so Naomi, her husband, and her two sons moved to Moab. Her sons both married, but over the next ten years, the sons and her husband died and all Naomi had left were her two daughters-in-law. Things continued to go downhill from there.

In biblical times it was considered a social and economic tragedy to lose your husband to death. If you were a childless widow, unable to provide for yourself, maintain the family estate, or pay off debts, you were dependent on other people and family members to meet your needs. All of Naomi's remaining blood relatives lived miles away in her hometown of Bethlehem. Her heart was surely crushed under the weight of her thoughts, feelings, and overwhelming emotions—anxiety, worry, stress, fear, grief, disappointment, sadness, anger, and hopelessness—and those feelings drove her attitudes and behaviors.

Naomi decided to return to Bethlehem as the country was rebounding from the famine, and her two widowed daughters-in-law, Orpah and Ruth, decided to go with her. But four miles into the journey, after Naomi apparently had plenty of time to process all of her circumstances and hardships, she stopped and encouraged the two women to turn back and remain in Moab. She said that she would travel to Bethlehem alone. Naomi went on to tell her daughters-in-law, "Things are far more bitter for me than for you, because the LORD himself has raised his fist against me" (Ruth 1:13). *The Message* translates this verse to say, "This is a bitter pill for me to swallow—more bitter for me than for you. God has dealt me a hard blow."

I can certainly relate to Naomi's feelings. Maybe you can too. When life deals us a hard blow, it's difficult not only to think positive but to stay positive. When the bank account is drained, a child is rebelling, a divorce becomes final, a loved one dies, a job ends, a friend betrays you, or a health problem strikes or worsens, it can seem utterly impossible to think positive thoughts. It's tempting to allow our circumstances to cause us to feel angry, frustrated, and bitter and to begin spewing our negativity to those around us. Naomi fell into that temptation, and her brewing bad attitude had only just begun.

Orpah turned back toward Moab, but Ruth stayed with Naomi and the two continued on their nearly sixty-mile journey, which was filled with treacherous terrain. As they walked and walked, day after day, I imagine Naomi had lots of time to think and mentally replay all of the heartache and loss she had endured.

And remember, whatever we focus our thoughts on will always grow in our minds.

Upon Naomi's arrival into Bethlehem, we see evidence of this overthinking in the bitterness of Naomi's words:

> So the two of them continued on their journey. When they came to Bethlehem, the entire town was excited by their arrival. "Is it really Naomi?" the women asked.
>
> "Don't call me Naomi," she responded. "Instead, call me Mara, for the Almighty has made life very bitter for me. I went away full, but the LORD has brought me home empty. Why call me Naomi when the LORD has caused me to suffer and the Almighty has sent such tragedy upon me?" (Ruth 1:19–21)

Instead of embracing her friends when they all ran up to welcome her back home, Naomi quickly spewed her negativity, informing them not to call her Naomi, but to call her Mara instead. Hebrew in origination, the name *Mara* means "bitter."[2] Naomi's negative thoughts not only caused her heart to become bitter, but they also influenced her to go so far as to change her name to bitterness, just to make her negativity official!

Naomi had every right to feel angry, abandoned, rejected, unprotected, uncared for, and unfairly burdened in life. After all, life wasn't what she had expected and her heartaches were many. If God hadn't caused her tragedies, He had certainly allowed them. She loved God and her faith had been strong, but now she felt unseen by Him. Unloved. Her new name personified the status of her new opinion about herself, her life, and her God. Naomi had been on an expedition back to the Promised Land, but her negativity cost her big-time. Physically she arrived in the city of Bethlehem, but mentally she arrived on the shore of toxic negativity.

I have found myself on that same shore, and maybe you have too. It's not a fun place to be. My desire to avoid landing there again is exactly what compels me to want to hang on to hope and to put my faith in God, even when life deals a hard blow.

The Cost to Our Health and Well-Being

Like Naomi, we may think we are justified in being upset or negative, and consequently we can become blinded to the toll it is taking. Negative thinking not only hurts our relationships, those around us, and our attitudes, it also affects our bodies. When we choose to think negative thoughts, we push our bodies into a state of physical and mental stress and distress. What we all too often fail to realize is that negativity can actually be physically detrimental as well. I know that to be true, because I've been there.

A few years ago, when I was writing my book *Stressed-Less Living: Finding God's Peace in Your Chaotic World*, I did a lot of research on the effects of stress on our bodies and our faith. It was then that I learned the profound connection between the health of our minds and the health of our bodies. I had experienced an enormous amount of stress in a difficult job that had landed me in various doctors' offices over and over, trying to find someone who could diagnose the cause of a myriad of issues, including vision problems, gastrointestinal problems, fatigue, headaches, insomnia, and heart palpitations. Months went by before I realized all my problems were rooted in my stress level, which was being fueled by the waves of negative thoughts raging through my mind every day.

The American Medical Association reports that 75 percent of all illnesses—from the common cold to cancer—in addition to 75 to 98 percent of all visits to primary care physicians, can be linked back to stress-related factors in the patients' lives. That was a real wake-up call for me![3]

My mind and all my overthinking and worrying were not only making me stressed but also tearing my body down little by little. I finally made some positive changes in my life, and most importantly in my faith walk, and began to earnestly seek God's peace. I realized I didn't have any power to control what was going on in my work environment, but I did have the power to control my thoughts and my reactions to those circumstances. I could choose to let my job steal my joy and let my attitude turn negative and sour, or I could choose to seek peace and joy in Christ. As the old saying goes, I asked God to calm the storm in me.

That season of life was difficult and a test of faith, and although I didn't change my name to Mara, at times I was tempted to! Fortunately, my eyes had been opened to the cost of my negative thoughts on my health. Even before I was able to make a change in my employment, I knew I had to make the choice to be positive on a daily, moment-by-moment basis, just like that sweet elderly lady in the nursing home, or my health would continue to suffer. When I asked God to change my heart and help me transform and renew my mind, my stress level diminished. As a result of my commitment to control my thoughts as well as to make some changes regarding work, every single one of my health problems eventually receded—without medication or treatment.

You Choose What You Gain or Lose

Dr. Caroline Leaf, a cognitive neuroscientist with a PhD in communication pathology specializing in neuropsychology, wrote a popular book titled *Switch On Your Brain*. In it she reveals that because we are constantly reacting to circumstances and events, our brains become shaped by the process of thoughts and reactions. If we think positively, the physiological aspects of our brains change in healthy ways that help us move toward a positive quality of life. Yet if we think negatively, our brains are changed in unhealthy ways, causing us to feel and act negatively, which steers us toward a more negative quality of life. This cycle shapes and designs our brains and, consequently, affects the health of our minds and bodies. Leaf also found that people who regularly meditate on Scripture and have developed a disciplined and focused thought life have increased intelligence, wisdom, and a feeling of peace.[4]

Until I read Leaf's book, I never knew my thinking could actually physically shape my brain and cause me to be more apt to being negative or positive. I love how this research supports what we are told in Scripture repeatedly: we can transform and renew our minds if we choose to (Rom. 12:2).

For all who struggle with negativity, pessimism, and even depression, this is good news! Although in many cases there are physiological reasons for depression, and therefore medication is beneficial and necessary, sometimes depression can be minimized when positive thinking becomes the norm instead of the exception.

When I was still struggling in the aftermath of my marriage breaking up, there were days I didn't want to get out of bed. Days when I would pull the covers up to my nose and stare aimlessly at the television for hours, my broken heart consumed with thoughts of despair and mourning. Days when I either couldn't stop crying or found myself always on the verge of tears. Days when I deliberately tried to avoid social gatherings, even with people I loved, and doing things I loved to do, like dining out, shopping, or just going to play tennis with friends, which is my favorite hobby.

But over time, the more I sought God's peace, the more I became equipped to control my thinking and be more positive and trusting of His plans for my life. I deliberately reframed my thoughts and surrendered my fears. I focused on my faith, prayed, and memorized mind-renewing Scripture verses. Gradually my thinking changed. The more I controlled my thoughts, the more control I had over my life. Before too long I noticed a drastic change in my attitude. My depression lifted. I had fervently sought after God, and when I did, He stepped in, came to my rescue, and helped me stop sinking in my faith, in my thoughts, and in my life.

Choose to Turn Around

My friend, when we allow our minds to be consumed with negativity and pessimism, we lose so much. But we don't have to live out our lives in negativity. It's never too late to start taking control of our thoughts and emotions and begin steering our minds, and our lives, in a whole new direction. Once we take that U-turn, God can radically change our perspectives and attitudes. What we think about the most drives our attitudes. As we think, so will we be.

God loves His own and listens intently and tenderly to the cries of His children. Psalm 34:15 reminds us of that promise: "The eyes of the LORD are on the righteous, and his ears are attentive to their cry" (NIV). *The Message* words it to say, "His ears pick up every moan and groan."

No matter how much you are hurting, how angry you are at your situation, how unfair you think God is being in your life, how forgotten you feel, how much moaning and groaning you do, please know this: God still listens, hears, and catches every tear. He loves you, nonetheless—without question. And He can redeem and restore our minds, our hearts, and our lives.

Eventually even Naomi's perspective and attitude changed for the better, and her life was positively redirected because of her faith. Her daughter-in-law Ruth ended up marrying a man named Boaz, and they soon had a son. Naomi had the blessing of living with them and helping raise their little boy. I love how we see that, although Naomi's optimism and attitude were shaken because of her hardships and losses, God's love for her was never shaken. Despite her discouragement and negativity, she stood in her faith and gradually God wove restoration back into her life. She eventually reclaimed her optimism and even her birth name. Bitter Mara disappeared, and pleasant Naomi returned.

Sweet friend, God can receive all of our anger, sadness, and raw emotions as any loving father will do for his own children. So it's okay to feel mad at Him for a time, to rant about our feelings, frustrations, and pain. It's okay to feel that life has treated us unfairly and to feel desperate for God to do something. It's natural to sometimes doubt whether He sees what we're enduring or cares about what we're going through. It's okay to acknowledge and admit we are stuck in a pit of negativity and pessimism. All these are reasonable human emotions.

But it's not okay to get stuck there. The cost of negativity is high. We may lose our relationships, our health, and our ability to be a blessing and a positive role model to others. However, when we release our burdens and the negativity that clings to them to the One who hears every moan and groan of our lips, we gain life, joy, health, and happiness.

Ask God to transform and renew your mind. He is ready to do so. No matter how much your faith has been shaken because of negative circumstances or perspectives, His love for you has never changed and He wants what is best for you: a positive mind and a positive life.

STRATEGIES FOR TRANSFORMING YOUR THINKING

Mind-Transforming Reflections

- As you think about the areas of your heart where you're tempted to focus on negative thinking, what's at risk? Specifically, are there relationships you value that are being harmed by your negativity or pessimistic outlook?

- Naomi suffered the heartbreaking loss of her husband and her two sons. She announced to her daughters-in-law, "Things are far more bitter for me than for you, because the LORD himself has raised his fist against me" (Ruth 1:13). She even asked her friends to call her "bitter"! Naomi *spoke* the negativity that had been bred in her heart. As you've been paying attention to your negative thoughts, which ones have you spoken aloud? Is there someone in particular who receives the bulk of your negativity? Write down the negative thoughts that you have spoken aloud, offering each one to the Lord. Don't condemn yourself; just ask God for an acute awareness of when they enter your mind next time, and the inner strength to try to say something positive instead.

- Are your eyes being opened to what you have lost or what you could lose as a result of negative thinking? Sometimes what we lose is internal, like peace, joy, and purpose. Other times we lose what is external, like relationships or opportunities. As you consider what's inside of you and what's outside of you, what have you lost? What could you lose?

- Tracie shared that negative thinking can affect our bodies. Close your eyes and take notice of each part of your body. Are you carrying stress in your neck? Shoulders? Does negativity pool in your gut? Do you carry your burdens in your back? Invite God to join you in a prayerful examination of your frame, and begin to recognize how you "carry" negativity and how it might be affecting you more than you have realized until now.

Mind-Renewing Memory Verses

Write out the verses below in your journal, or on your notecards, and commit them to memory.

> The eyes of the LORD are on the righteous,
> and his ears are attentive to their cry.
> (Ps. 34:15 NIV)

> And we know that God causes everything to work together for the good of those who love God and are called according to his purpose for them. (Rom. 8:28)

No, in all these things we are more than conquer-
ors through him who loved us. (Rom. 8:37 NIV)

So after you have suffered a little while, he will
restore, support, and strengthen you, and he will
place you on a firm foundation. (1 Pet. 5:10)

You can pray for anything, and if you have faith,
you will receive it. (Matt. 21:22)

(If you have time, consider reading the four chapters of the
book of Ruth and invite God to further speak to your heart
through her story.)

Chapter Challenge

Think of people you may avoid because of their pessimism and negativity. Write down what you think their negativity has cost them.

Think of people you love to be around because of their optimism and joy. People who make you feel happy when you are with
them and after you leave their presence. Write down what you
admire about them and how their optimism has brought blessings into their lives and yours. Of these two people you've written
about, can you see the difference their attitude has made in their
lives? Who do you most want to be like in your own life?

Now write down three things you can do in the next week
to begin living out your commitment to let God transform your

mind. Make these really practical and applicable in your specific circumstances and with the people in your life. Here are a few examples:

- Compliment the coworker I despise.
- Express gratitude to a parent with whom I struggle.
- Praise someone of whom I'm typically most critical.
- Speak kindly to others of someone who gets on my last nerve.
- Come up with two positive benefits that could result from an adversity I'm currently facing.

Throughout the week, record any blessings or benefits—to you or to others—you see from doing this activity.

Don't just let the devil use your mind as a garbage dump.

Joyce Meyer

Chapter Four

WHO WE ARE, AND WHO WE ARE NOT

Surfacing Misconceptions

Life-robbing misconceptions are lies that
keep us bound. They spring up from
the way we interpret our experience,
not the actual experience itself.

He may have never thought about me again, but I thought about him every single day for quite some time.

I had been working at a job I loved for five years when I was assigned a new supervisor. Although I had had a successful track record, my first performance review with this new supervisor made it clear that meeting his expectations was going to be difficult. Even the smallest mistakes or shortcomings were magnified under the microscope of his criticism. But I humbly took his suggestions, thanked him for the constructive feedback, and became determined to make sure I met or exceeded every single one of his expectations over the next year.

Twelve months flew by, and even though my stress level was through the roof, and my health was declining as a result, I gave my job all I had, keeping meticulous notes of my accomplishments and the goals I'd met. I walked into the next performance review feeling prepared, confident, and proud. I walked out of that performance review stinging from the unkindness of his words. They swirled in my mind for days in a torrential current.

"You're not working enough hours or overtime."

"Just because you think you met that goal doesn't mean you did it the right way."

"You can't be a good mother and a career woman and excel at both."

"Your male coworker can do this better and without any mistakes. Why can't you?"

"You're too quiet in meetings and don't contribute enough."

"You're too nice to people when it comes to handling conflicts. A successful manager needs to be stern and without emotion."

"You should have taken a different approach on this project and done it better."

"Why can't you figure out this accounting software? It's not that hard."

"You should have done more …"

This is merely a tiny sampling of the dozens of personal insults this man dumped onto my heart for three hours that day, leaving me feeling incompetent, broken, defeated, and hopelessly flawed in every regard. This manager criticized everything I had done or not done for an entire year, highlighting every perceived flaw, imperfection, and weakness, and in the wake of his unfair critique I was left feeling as if I had no value whatsoever. All the insecurities and negative thoughts I'd ever battled abruptly resurfaced in the wake of his harsh, unkind judgment. Soon after that devastating evaluation, I resigned from my position.

While I knew God had been calling me to a new plan and purpose for my life, and my faith allowed me to believe I could trust in His ways, the impact of this supervisor's wounding words lingered. Specifically, his criticism of my work performance gave birth to misconceptions about my identity. Even though I acknowledged and accepted the areas in which I needed to improve, overall I felt rejected, worthless, and expendable and began to entertain false beliefs that were attached to those feelings—beliefs such as these:

> I'm not worthy.
>
> I'm not smart.
>
> I'm not a good enough mom/wife/human being.
>
> I'll never succeed.
>
> I have no future.
>
> God doesn't care about me.
>
> I have no identity now that I'm unemployed.

At first, I didn't recognize the ways this man's words had morphed inside me. I didn't notice that his opinions had mutated, like cancerous cells, into sweeping generalizations about my value that I had come to accept as true. But as I sank—suffering under the weight of my own hurt, outrage, resentment, and feelings of unworthiness—God began to show me the misconceptions that were bringing me down and burying my self-esteem, my attitude, and my happiness.

Lies Keep Us Bound

Life-robbing misconceptions are lies that keep us bound. They thwart us from becoming all that God has made us to be and keep us from living in the peace and happiness we were designed to enjoy. These misconceptions are often rooted in the tiniest sliver of truth—a childhood wound, a loss beyond our control, a rejection, a sin from the past. They spring up from the way we interpret that experience, not the actual experience itself, and grow into full-blown lies about who we are and who God is.

For example:

- A woman whose teenage son is using drugs believes, *This is all my fault. I'm a terrible mother.*
- A person working in an office where she feels disliked and unappreciated surmises, *My circumstances are the cause of my unhappiness, and I have no control over how I feel.*

- A woman whose husband has cheated on her deduces, *I'm not enough as a woman or a wife, and I never will be.*

- A woman who loses her father and mother in a span of six months concludes, *God must be punishing me and trying to teach me something.*

- A woman who is single and would prefer to be married tells herself, *I guess I don't deserve to be happy. God will never bring someone into my life.*

- A woman whose father didn't love her as a child believes, *I am not lovable or worthy to be loved.*

- A victim of childhood abuse believes, *I am damaged goods and don't have any value. I should live in secret shame of what was done to me.*

When we're tangled up in one of these life-robbing misconceptions, we're not able to distinguish the difference between our experiences and our interpretations of those experiences and the meaning we've given to them. Our misconceptions keep us stuck, unable to live the life of joy and peace we long for.

Graciously, though, God will reveal to us the misconceptions we've believed, so that we can learn to overcome them and find life-giving freedom. As I made my faith a priority and began to focus on what God said about me instead of my supervisor's opinion, God's love and acceptance gave me the courage to push past my hurt, embrace who I was in Him, and believe He had a beautiful plan and purpose for my life. I began to spend more and more time in His Word, making my faith and my trust in Him a priority. Gradually, I rediscovered that my value, my identity, and my worth as a person was in Him and Him alone. I learned that my value isn't tied to a person, position, salary, accomplishment, or a met goal. It isn't tied to being the perfect wife, mom, friend, or sister. It isn't tied to what I do for God, or what I don't do for God. My value is only tied to the cross, where Jesus thought I was valuable enough to die for. He died for you as well, because you too are valuable to Him.

Refusing to Harbor Misconceptions

Regardless if you don't like what you see when you look in the mirror and your past haunts you or present experiences or hurtful people are chipping away at your self-confidence, know that most of us harbor misconceptions about our identities and our value. But in God's strength, it's also possible to reject those misconceptions and refuse to let them steal our joy any longer.

I love the story in Matthew 15 about a woman who refused to listen to what other people said and thought about her, and instead chose to believe she was worthy in Jesus's eyes. Jesus had left Galilee and was headed north to the region of Tyre and Sidon when He came across this woman. She was a Gentile, and that fact alone caused a lot of Jews to view her as worthless, unimportant, and inferior; but she didn't let their opinion of her, or any self-doubt, grow into misconceptions that would thwart her.

The woman begged Jesus to deliver her daughter from a demon possession, but He appeared to rebuke her, while the disciples pleaded with Him to send her away. "But Jesus gave her no reply, not even a word. Then his disciples urged him to send her away. 'Tell her to go away,' they said. 'She is bothering us with all her begging'" (Matt. 15:23).

That was the ancient way of saying, "She's getting on our nerves and doesn't deserve your attention!" It's easy to imagine that this woman might have been crushed by their rejection. In fact, even Jesus seemed to reject her, announcing that He'd come not for the Gentiles but for Israel. When the woman pleaded for His help, Jesus resisted again, saying, "It isn't right to take food from the children and throw it to the dogs" (Matt. 15:26). Though the woman clearly had a lot of internal fortitude, that one had to hurt. In ancient times dogs were considered worthless pests. Unfazed, the woman—convinced that her daughter was worth saving and convinced that Jesus could save her—challenged Him, "That's true, Lord, but even dogs are allowed to eat the scraps that fall beneath their masters' table" (Matt. 15:27).

As the two of them looked at each other in silence, with the jeers of the crowd and the disciples in the background, this woman could have been overcome, absorbing the taunts of the crowd who believed she was an inferior person in their society. She could have become consumed with what everyone thought of her and slunk away in humiliation and shame. She could have hidden her face, embarrassed at how her daughter behaved as a result of being demon possessed. She could have apologized for even imagining that Jesus would care about her and her daughter, mentally beating herself up for being so stupid. She could have stiffened up in anger and backed away, offended by the confusing and seemingly critical response she at first received to her plea.

But instead she stood firm in her faith. She rejected the lies about who she was or who her daughter was. Ignoring the voices that demeaned her, she clung to God's truth. She was bold, and Jesus responded to her boldness, affirming her faith and healing her daughter. "'Dear woman,' Jesus said to her, 'your faith is great. Your request is granted'" (Matt. 15:28). And her daughter was instantly healed. As a result, this Canaanite woman was one of the first Gentiles to enter the kingdom of God.

Unearthing and Rejecting What Binds

I imagine, like me, you've also had experiences that have left your heart drenched with hurt, insecurity, or negativity. Perhaps you've suffered from the words or actions of a parent, coworker, spouse, sibling, or friend. Maybe you were a victim of physical, emotional, or mental abuse that shook your confidence to the core and stole your self-worth. It might be that failures or poor choices have left you convinced you have no value, much less that you're valuable in God's eyes.

Unearthing and then rejecting misconceptions about who we are always leads to freedom. I want to tell you about three women I know—Patricia, Melissa, and Cara—who lived shackled and bound for years by misconceptions, but who are now experiencing peace and joy because they unearthed and rejected those misconceptions.

Patricia's earthly father was very critical of her throughout her childhood. She could never please him or gain his approval. He constantly let her know she was not living up to his expectations, many of which were unfair and unrealistic. When she became an adult, he rejected her and shut her out of his life completely. Consequently, Patricia grew to believe the lies of the enemy that love, acceptance, and promises were conditional, no matter who they came from. To protect herself, she erected barriers around her heart. Since her own father didn't love her, Patricia deduced that she would never be good enough for any man and that men would always let her down. When other prayers seemed to go unanswered, she began to believe the misconception that God was letting her down too. These misconceptions prevented her from loving her husband, her Savior, and her life.

However, God never turned His back on Patricia. He used various Christian women to speak truth and hope into her life. As she grew in her faith, God's Word began to penetrate her deepest hurts. He softened her heart and revealed ways the misconceptions she was beginning to notice were harming her and her marriage. Eyes opened, Patricia began to trust God, and as she released the old misconceptions, she eventually started to trust her husband and his love for her too.

Melissa had always been self-conscious about living with a physical disability. As a result, she embraced the misconception that she wasn't valuable or beautiful or capable of embracing God's good purpose for her life. Over time Melissa realized that she had developed a "woe is me" disposition and was paying a high price to live under the shadow of negativity: she'd gained nothing and had lost peace, joy, self-confidence, and healthy relationships.

Through a mentoring relationship with a Christian counselor, Melissa was able to unearth some of the negative thoughts she'd been holding on to. In time she was able to reject them and stop letting them steal her happiness. That release also made room for her to receive and embrace the love God had for her. Because she'd opened that door, Melissa began to live with confidence, purpose, and vision, and she broke the habit of thinking pessimistic, critical thoughts about herself.

At three hundred pounds, Cara thought her weight was the reason for her unhappiness. She felt all the things that were wrong with her life were tied to the number on the scale, and that if she could lose weight, then she could be happy and positive. One day through faith, she realized that the lies she had believed about herself were holding her hostage, bound to the lies Satan was telling her. God opened her eyes to see that the problem was her way of thinking, not her obesity. She began intentionally filling her mind with what God's Word said about her, instead of the negative thoughts that had been causing her to sink. I love how she describes the moment her life turned around: "I used to think my weight was my problem. But God showed me the real problem was me (my thinking). Once I got out of my own way and started following His lead, my life drastically changed."

Cara decided to take control of her thoughts, which equipped her to take back her life, which included going on a successful weight-loss journey for eighteen months. She says that to everyone else it just looked like she'd lost weight, but she knows it meant much more. The weight loss demonstrated that she had finally broken the chains of negativity and self-condemnation. She had broken free of them, and God not only redeemed her thoughts, He redeemed her life.

What Have You Believed?

As I type these words, I'm imagining the kinds of hurtful words, criticism, rejection, or actions you may have endured from those whose approval, love, and acceptance you needed most.

Maybe like Patricia, Melissa, and Cara you've spent years feeling inferior because of the misconceptions you've believed.

Maybe, like me, you have invisible scars from the wounds of critical and hurtful words spoken to you. Maybe it was a parent or another family member who inflicted those scars. Maybe it was a boss or coworker or colleague. Maybe it was a teacher, neighbor, friend, pastor, or fellow church member.

Maybe you secretly see yourself as a "dog," an inferior human compared to everyone else in the world. (Don't we all feel "less than" more frequently than we'd like to admit?) If so, then Satan has been hard at work on your heart and mind, fueling self-condemnation in an effort to destroy your self-esteem. But listen up. You do not have to let him have the last say. You have the power in you as a child of God to choose the thoughts you will entertain.

If you've been suffocating under misconceptions about your value, I believe God's heart has been breaking for you. And I also believe that there's hope for Him to change your mind and free your heart from the bondage of negativity.

The Beauty of Freedom

I had finished speaking at a retreat over the weekend, and the time had come to encourage the women to surrender the lies and negative misconceptions that had been holding them hostage. Following my instructions, they each took out the white notecards I had placed on their seats and began to write down the false beliefs they wanted to surrender to God. Misconceptions they wanted to be freed from once and for all. As soft music played, some wept silently as they scrawled out their deepest insecurities; others walked up to the front of the room and knelt as they dropped their white notecards onto the altar. Woman after woman surrendered the lies she had believed.

After the event was over and the room was empty, I stayed behind to collect the hundreds of notecards scattered around the room. Later in my hotel room, I dumped them out onto the bed and began to sift through them, reading each notecard one by one. The cards revealed a broad spectrum of lies many women carry in their hearts.

> "I had an abortion and God will never forgive me."
> "Nobody really cares about me, and I don't matter to anyone."
> "I could never forgive my family for hurting me."

"I'm so ashamed of my divorce and think God
hates me for it."
"I'm depressed and I can never be happy."
"My husband discarded me for a younger woman,
and I feel worthless."

As I read, I prayed for each woman, whose name I didn't know
but whom God knew intimately. Tears fell into my lap as I came
face to face with a tidal wave of lies and misconceptions the enemy
had woven deep into the hearts of these beautiful women.

"I can never trust people again because I've been
hurt too many times."
"Church is full of hypocritical people, and I've
pulled away from church."
"If people knew the real me, the sins of my past,
they wouldn't like me anymore."
"I struggle with gluttony. I'm ashamed of
my weight but feel I can never overcome the
addiction to eating."
"I'm mad at God because He gave me this
disease."
"My circumstances will never change, and God
doesn't really care about me."

No one would ever guess by looking at these women that they
were suffering so much on the inside. They had come to the retreat

wearing smiles, cute new outfits, and a facade of confidence, yet many were secretly broken and scarred by life. Tears of happiness flowed as I considered how God would be working in their hearts going forward, now that they had fresh hope and freedom. God can do the same for you.

Now when I think back to the way my boss's words hurt me, I'm reminded of a quote I've heard my whole life: "Nobody can make you feel inferior without your consent." As we notice and capture the misconceptions we've believed, we retract our consent to feel inferior! Today I live with so much more freedom because I've learned how to identify some of the wily beliefs that have kept me bound. I'm no longer blown about by the words or actions of others, and I no longer allow misconceptions and lies from the enemy to keep me from believing in my own self-worth and value and who I am in Christ.

One of the greatest things we can do for ourselves is to notice the negative thoughts and misconceptions that have robbed us of our peace and joy. As we notice the lies we've believed, we take the reins from others—from those around us, from the enemy—and hand them back to God. The Gentile woman who boldly approached Jesus was unwilling to buy into the opinions of others. She knew that her daughter was *worth* healing, and she knew who had the power to do it. As we imitate her spirit, and hang on to what's most true, we can experience the life we long for.

The deceiver's strategy is to capitalize from our insecurities and doubts, distort our thinking, and steal our joy. When he lies, it is consistent with his character; for he is a liar and the father of lies (John 8:44). But God is faithful to surface the misconceptions and lies that have anchored us in negativity, doubt, and despair. Granted, we'll still have to deal with the words and actions that once dragged us under, and new hurtful words might be spoken. But unsinkable faith can be ours as we purpose to expose and release the misconceptions that keep us stuck. As we continue to journey together, we'll discover how to replace these lies with the truth—and with God's truths. For now, you're gaining real traction by exposing the misconceptions that have kept you stuck.

STRATEGIES FOR TRANSFORMING YOUR THINKING

Mind-Transforming Reflections

- Often when we're tangled up in misconceptions, we interpret another's behavior to be about *us* and not them. The unkindness and bad behavior of Tracie's boss was all about him, but for years Tracie believed that his actions defined *her*. Record some of the hurts and tender places in your heart that are connected to some of the adult relationships in your life *today*—perhaps a spouse, a sibling, a friend, an enemy. Beside each, note what is yours to carry and what belongs to the other person. Prayerfully offer these thoughts and insecurities to God. When those old misconceptions are triggered, choose for truth and continue to release them.

- Because of a father who was ill equipped to love her well, Patricia believed she wasn't worth loving. As you think about your parents—ones who were present and ones who were absent—what are the lies you've believed as a result of your relationship? Make a list of these misconceptions as the Spirit allows them to surface. Offer them to God.

- Melissa, who suffered with misconceptions about her worth, found freedom through a mentoring relationship with a Christian counselor. God is often gracious to use qualified ministry professionals to help us get unstuck! Have you enjoyed the fruit of this kind of relationship?

If not, and you feel it would be beneficial, write out a prayer to God, asking that if it is His will, He might open the door for you to be in a relationship with a therapist, pastor, or a mature Christian who can journey with you through this season of healing.

- The Gentile woman who begged God to heal her daughter protested, "Even dogs are allowed to eat the scraps that fall beneath their masters' table" (Matt. 15:27). Culturally shamed, she knew that most Jews saw her as a "dog." Is there a negative word that doesn't tell the truth about who you are but has stuck in your spirit? It might be a word that someone spoke aloud, or it might be a word you've assigned to yourself. Ask God to show you what false words you've held on to, and then release that word—and all the shame that goes with it—to God.

Mind-Renewing Memory Verses

Write out the verses below in your journal, or on your notecards, and commit them to memory.

> You know when I sit and when I rise;
> you perceive my thoughts from afar.
> (Ps. 139:2 NIV)

> He has always hated the truth, because there is no truth in him. When he lies, it is consistent with

his character; for he is a liar and the father of lies.
(John 8:44)

But God showed his great love for us by sending
Christ to die for us while we were still sinners.
(Rom. 5:8)

And the very hairs on your head are all numbered.
So don't be afraid; you are more valuable to God
than a whole flock of sparrows. (Luke 12:7)

God's way is perfect. All the LORD's promises
prove true. He is a shield for all who look to him
for protection. (Ps. 18:30)

Chapter Challenge

Pull out your journal and draw three columns, like the ones below.

What I Experienced	Misconceptions about Me	Misconceptions about God

In the left column, list some of the moments, experiences, or seasons that have changed your view of yourself or of God. For example, your list might include: "I was relinquished for adoption," "My grandma died," "My boyfriend cheated on me," "I suffered a miscarriage," "I got fired," "My husband left me for a younger woman." Then, beside each one, try to identify the misconception that grew in your heart as a result.

For instance, next to "My boss berated me," I'd note that I believed of myself, "I'm not worthy," and I believed about God, "God doesn't care for me because He let someone treat me that way."

My friend Mandy could write, "My mother died when I was three." And because I've journeyed with her, I know that she's grown to notice the lies she believed as a result: "I'm not worth sticking around for" and "God has abandoned me too."

As you review the misconceptions and negative thoughts that have grown in your heart, prayerfully release each one to God. If, like an irksome weed, the thought returns, simply root it out again and offer it to God. The best way to determine what's true and what's a lie is to observe what you've believed through the lens of God's Word. Regardless of how certain misconceptions were formed in your mind, if what you believe about yourself contradicts Scripture's revelation of who you are (beloved, worthy, cherished) or who God is (gracious, trustworthy, merciful), then you've been hoodwinked. Trust that God's Spirit delights in setting you free by exposing any of the lies you've believed.

As a single footstep will not make a path on the earth, so a
single thought will not make a pathway in the mind.
To make a deep physical path, we walk again and again.
To make a deep mental path, we must think over and over
the kind of thoughts we wish to dominate our lives.

Henry David Thoreau

Chapter Five

BREAKING THE HABIT

Capturing the ANTs in Our Heads

Each of us has the power to choose how we think. If we're
committed to doing the work, beginning with noticing
and capturing our negative thoughts, we can enjoy the
satisfaction, peace, and joy we were made for.

Negative thinking is nothing more than a bad habit, and bad habits are meant to be broken. This takes willpower, commitment, and faith. In the words of Joyce Meyer, if we want real change to happen in the battlefield of our minds, we have to have a backbone, not a wishbone![1]

You've likely heard it takes twenty-one days to break a habit, but research has proven that sometimes it takes a lot longer than that, and a lot of intentional effort. In fact, according to some studies, it can take anywhere from two to eight months to really get a new habit ingrained in your mind.[2] But don't let that discourage you! Elliott Berkman, neuroscientist and assistant professor from the University of Oregon, said, "People who want to kick their

[bad] habit for reasons that are aligned with their personal values will change their behaviour faster than people who are doing it for external reasons such as pressure from others."[3] Simply put, if something is important enough to us, especially if it aligns with our faith and our deepest desires for peace and a healthy, happy life, we are more likely to make the effort to change.

You may have come to believe happiness and peace are not attainable for you because of the adversities in your life, the fears in your heart, the skeletons in your closet, or the hurt you experienced in the past. Maybe you've allowed negative thinking to become part of who you are, as I once did, and deem it an impossible task to break the habit of negative thinking. But just as Jesus said in Matthew 19:26, "Humanly speaking, it is impossible. But with God everything is possible"—including breaking free from the bad habit of negativity.

God didn't say transformation would be quick or easy, much less that it would happen in twenty-one days. But when Paul offered, "Let God transform you into a new person by changing the way you think" (Rom. 12:2), God did promise that it could happen. When we wholeheartedly desire to be changed and transformed, God will work in us to make that change become a reality, so that one day we'll suddenly realize we no longer have to try to break the habit, because our faith has gently ushered us into a more positive mind-set and a more positive life.

We can't change how our attitude has been in the past, but we can change how our attitude will be in the future. Remember, being positive is a daily choice, not a destination. We will never "arrive" as a positive person, because life will continually give us reasons to be negative, throw us curveballs, or even seem like it's falling apart from time to time. When we learn to notice the thoughts that are driving our feelings and shift those thoughts to something more positive, we will be free from the whims of our emotions and live in the light of God's grace and sufficiency. The battle for your mind is one you can win—and it's well worth the fight.

Habit-Breaking Benefits

For months after Susan's husband left her, an insistent thought flooded her mind, *You are worthless garbage to be discarded. No man will ever love you.* The thought was upsetting to her, and when it captured her, she'd feel crushed, void of all hope for the future. In talking with a Christian counselor and after having spent time in God's Word, she finally began to notice the power this thought had over her. She knew, intellectually, that this was not God's truth. But it was as if the lie's talons had a grip on her.

One day Susan intentionally chose to start resisting those lies. Closing her eyes, she prayerfully paid attention to what she was telling herself. Each morning as she awoke to the reality that her husband was not waking up beside her, painful emotions would flood in and her thoughts would morph into feelings of how unworthy she felt. But instead of dwelling on those thoughts, Susan asked God to change her view of herself. She envisioned Him wrapping His arms around her and holding her tight, reassuring her of her value and worth in His eyes.

Gradually, as she did this day after day, she came back to life. She embraced her value in Christ and started to look forward to all the new beginnings God had in store for her. She memorized Scripture verses to recite when she was feeling down, ones that reminded her she was God's precious beloved, that He adored her, and that He had great plans for her future. Slowly, as Susan soaked in God's truths and allowed them to permeate the hurting places of her heart, her bereft and lonely heart began to come back to life. Today she says, "I am not worthless garbage to be discarded. I am God's beloved. I am treasured. I have value." Her bold faith in who she was changed not only her outlook and her attitude but also her life.

When we begin to think differently, we begin to feel differently, and eventually, we begin to live differently. You see, breaking free from the habit of negative thinking opens the door for new life to take root.

Oh, sweet friend, despite what has happened in your past, what circumstances you are facing, or how long you've struggled with the habit of negative thinking, God is ready to help you break that bad habit that is keeping you bound. If you've been thinking that since your circumstances are beyond your control there's little you can do to achieve peace and happiness, then I hope you're beginning to realize that is yet another lie from the deceiver. When you capture and reject the negative thoughts and perspectives that fill your mind, you can start to replace them with truth. The things you focus on will change, and so will you as you intentionally strive for unsinkable faith.

Our Thoughts Matter

God knew life would be hard, that we would mess up from time to time and even go down the wrong paths. He knew it would be difficult to keep a sound positive mind focused on the things that please Him as we face the adversities and heartaches of life, so He made it possible for us to transform and renew our minds. He made it possible for us to start over and start fresh from the inside out. If that is our hearts' desire, we can grow in our awareness of the thoughts keeping us bound and learn how to overcome them.

When I first read Dr. Daniel G. Amen's *New York Times* best-selling book, *Change Your Brain, Change Your Life*, I was inspired and encouraged by his conclusions and research. Amen not only brought to light the complexity of how God made our brains and how important brain health is to our lives, but he also confirmed that it is possible to live a life filled with positive thinking, even for those of us who have spent years weighted down with hard circumstances, painful memories, crushed dreams, negativity, and generalized pessimism.

Amen reported that scientists estimate our brains have one hundred billion cells, with each one connected to other cells, forming up to ten thousand individual connections. There are more connections in the brain than there are stars in the universe.[4] So it's not hard to understand why the brain, and those tens of thousands of thoughts we think every day, has such a huge impact on our moods, our emotions, our outlooks, and most importantly, our peace, happiness, and joy. As Dr. Amen pointed out, "If our thinking patterns are excessively negative, harsh, or critical, that will have a negative impact on our moods, anxiety levels, and, ultimately, our ability to focus."[5] In my own research about stress years ago, I learned that most emotional and physical symptoms of stress and depression are not typically caused by the circumstances themselves but by how our minds perceive what is going on and how our hearts hold up under the pressure. When our hearts are under pressure, our minds are as well.

What I loved about Dr. Amen's research was not just that he exposed the complex inner workings of the human brain as God created it, but how science agreed with the message of transformation and redemption presented in the Scriptures! Long before scientists were able to study and research how our brains work, God's Word was telling us how we can transform our minds. Romans 12:2 says, "Don't become so well-adjusted to your culture that you fit into it without even thinking. Instead, fix your attention on God. You'll be changed from the inside out" (THE MESSAGE).

So science is finally catching up to Scripture, and although the only real proof we need in order to believe God can renew and transform our minds is that God said so in Romans, if you've ever doubted you could transform your mind by changing the way you think, this might be the further proof you need to believe it's possible for you.

Crushing Negativity

I also loved the acronym that Amen shared in his book: ANT—automatic negative thoughts. He said that whenever we notice ANTs creeping into our minds, we need to crush them or else they'll multiply, just like one little ant in our kitchen sink turns into dozens of ants if we don't take care of it immediately. He recommended being aware of all the little negative thoughts that automatically come to our minds and then taking action to reject and replace them.

This is exactly what my friend Sheila is learning to do. She recently confided with me how she has always struggled with the habit of believing every negative, self-condemning thought that popped into her head—*I'm not pretty enough; I'm not smart enough; I can't do anything right; I have no talents or skills.* She constantly battles a running mental diatribe telling her no man will ever want her because she was abused as a child, and that no one is trustworthy. Sheila lives in fear of being real with others, because the hordes of ANTs in her head tell her that if people knew the real Sheila, they wouldn't like her and would probably talk about her behind her back. My heart broke as she shared these raw feelings, evidence of deep wounds in her spirit that have never fully healed.

But Sheila has seen how much the ANTs in her head have cost her and is committed to capturing them and crushing them in order to break free of the habit of negativity. She wants to stop letting the false beliefs in her head become realities in her life. In the past, Sheila's thoughts had always had power—and a negative strong hold—over her life, but now she consciously and intentionally chooses to fight back every day. Her commitment to change will help her to one day achieve victory in her thinking habits, but just the fact that she is taking a step toward intentionally becoming a more positive thinker has already changed her life. When we admit our need for change and ask God to help us overcome the habit of negativity, we are able to break free and fully embrace the life of optimism and joy He offers.

The Process That Works

Even if she didn't realize it at the time, by capturing her ANTS, Sheila was implementing an essential step in the transforming of her mind. These three simple steps have been instrumental in my life as I've learned that they truly do work, and I know they can be instrumental in yours too.

1. *Notice negative thoughts*

Ask God to expose each negative thought you have. You take authority over your thoughts when you notice the ones you've allowed and begin to recognize the thinking patterns that have developed in your mind over time. Noticing and capturing the thoughts that have kept you bound is the first step in transformation.

2. *Reject negative thoughts*

After you notice a negative thought, you have the power to reject it. Refuse to entertain it in your mind or on your lips. Reject any thought that lies about who you are, who others are, or who God is. If what you are thinking doesn't line up with Scripture, it is not true. Toss out any thought that makes you feel hopeless, worried, or afraid. When you're tempted to complain, blame, or shame, use the power God has given you to refrain. When you reject negative thoughts, they lose their power over you.

3. *Replace negative thoughts*

Each time you exterminate a negative thought that's been exposed, replace it with a thought that is *more true*.

For example: Notice the negative thought *No one really loves me* and replace it with *There are people who love me, but most importantly, I am God's beloved*. Or notice the negative thought *I always mess things up*, and replace it with *I'm human and sometimes fail, but I'm not a failure and I can succeed*. Or *I'll never be able to lose the weight/overcome the addiction/find someone to love me* with *All things are possible with Christ*.

At first this may feel awkward or forced or even artificial. (Your brain might not be used to claiming and announcing what's true!) As you continue to choose what's most true, though, your brain begins to form new neural pathways that strengthen God's renewal and transformation of your mind.

I also want to suggest a tool that will help you as you notice, reject, and replace your negative thoughts. Journal a record of the thoughts you exterminate each day, in an effort to begin recognizing patterns of habitual negative thinking. Beside each one, note the thought you're choosing to replace the negative one with. Keeping track will also help you recognize when you are beginning to think differently and on the cusp of breaking free from the stronghold that certain negative thoughts have had over your life.

When It's Hard

In her book *Battlefield of the Mind*, Joyce Meyer wrote, "Being positive in a positive situation is easy. Anyone can do that. But, when we are positive in a negative situation it shows a genuine trust in God and a spiritual maturity that pleases and glorifies God."[6] Life is not always going to be positive, and difficult circumstances may seem to constantly roll in like waves, but as we seek God's help to transform our thinking habits, we can learn how to be positive in negative situations. And when we think like God, we will act in a more pleasing way to Him, and as a result, He will be glorified.

Colossians 3:1–2 says this: "So if you're serious about living this new resurrection life with Christ, act like it. Pursue the things over which Christ presides. Don't shuffle along, eyes to the ground, absorbed with the things right in front of you. Look up, and be alert to what is going on around Christ—that's where the action is. See things from his perspective" (THE MESSAGE). The apostle Paul is saying that we choose what we see and how we see! Dr. Amen exhorts, "We can live in a hell of our own making, or we can live in a heaven of our own making."[7] We can continue to wallow in our negative thoughts, or we can dig in and identify and reject them. Then as we replace negative thoughts with positive ones, our entire life experience is transformed. Simply put: *our lives are better*—even if our circumstances stay the same. Our thoughts, not our circumstances, are what will determine our happiness.

The choice is ours. My friend, I can't say it too many times: we all have the power to control our thoughts and the opportunity to live a peace-filled, happy life despite our circumstances; we just have to choose to take control. Our thoughts have power, but it is always up to us what thoughts we give power to.

Breaking the Habit

As you begin noticing and rejecting your negative thoughts, you are on your way to being able to replace them. The more you do this, the more natural it will become. What began with concerted effort and intentionality will become something you do without even thinking about it.

God is offering you a beautiful gift. It is yours for the taking.

When you change the way you look at things, the things you look at will change. So will you. Freedom from negative thinking will fling open the door for your new life to begin as you grow spiritually and strive for unsinkable faith.

God is faithful to show us the misconceptions that have anchored us in negativity, doubt, and despair. Releasing the misconceptions we've held doesn't mean that the rest of our lives will be smooth sailing. Storms will still come. Skies will thunder. Lightning will strike. Waves will inevitably rock our boats. We'll still have to deal with the words and actions of others that once dragged us under. But unsinkable faith can be ours as we purpose to expose and release the misconceptions that have kept us stuck. In the next chapter we'll take a closer look at how you can retrain your mind to think positive thoughts. Guided by the Spirit, you and I have all the tools we need to *live well.*

STRATEGIES FOR TRANSFORMING YOUR THINKING

Mind-Transforming Reflections

- Susan experienced a transformed life when she worked hard at breaking her bad habit of negative thinking and recognizing the lies she was listening to. It is God's good pleasure to expose the lies of the enemy. Has there been a formational experience in your life—perhaps several—that seeded your heart with lies about who you are or who God is? You've already been working hard to notice and expose the thoughts and lies that are keeping you bound. Ask God to shine light on any remaining lies that need to be exposed. Record these in your journal.

- Remember Romans 12:2: "Don't copy the behavior and customs of this world, but let God transform you into a new person by changing the way you think." As God continues to transform your mind, pay attention to the ways your mind has been and is affected by your culture. Do you have negative friends or family members? Do you watch risqué television or frequently see movies with content that wouldn't be pleasing to God? Listen to song lyrics with foul language or meanings? Have a spouse or coworker who is a chronic complainer? Follow people on social media who constantly post inappropriate or negative content? Note in your journal the influences that may be affecting your thinking. Beside each one, jot a simple action plan for how to avoid them. Regardless of who might be a negative influence in your life, commit to filtering the complaints you hear while praying for God to guard your heart, and try to be a positive influence in their lives (optimism is contagious you know!).

- Got ANTs? This week use your journal, or an app on your phone, to record your automatic negative thoughts. (You should have started this list in chapter 1.) There is power in training your brain to notice these!

Mind-Renewing Memory Verses

Write out the verses below in your journal, or on your notecards, and commit them to memory.

> Think about the things of heaven, not the things of earth. (Col. 3:2)

> Jesus looked at them intently and said, "Humanly speaking, it is impossible. But with God everything is possible." (Matt. 19:26)

This means that anyone who belongs to Christ has become a new person. The old life is gone; a new life has begun! (2 Cor. 5:17)

Seek the Kingdom of God above all else, and live righteously, and he will give you everything you need. (Matt. 6:33)

Instead, let the Spirit renew your thoughts and attitudes. (Eph. 4:23)

Chapter Challenge

Continue recognizing your negative thoughts, but also begin to reject them and replace them with God's truths. This is a critical part of capturing your thoughts and making them captive to Christ so your mind can begin to transform, renew, and change.

Spend a few moments in prayer, asking God to make you aware of the negative thoughts that habitually threaten your peace and joy. Open your heart to hear His voice, and ask for the spiritual insight to know when He is quickening your spirit.

Then pull out your journal and draw three columns like the following ones.

NOTICE Negative Thought	REJECT (exterminate) What is probably truer and more realistic	REPLACE One applicable, relevant, positive truth from Scripture to apply and remember
I can never do anything right.	I can't do everything right, but I can do a lot of things right.	"God has made us what we are. He has created us in Christ Jesus to live lives filled with good works that he has prepared for us to do" (Eph. 2:10 GW).

In the left-hand column, write down the negative thought you often struggle with. In the middle column, record something that is probably truer than what you are telling yourself. Then in the right-hand column, record a Scripture verse, truth, phrase, or promise from God's Word that disputes the negative thought you're entertaining.

Here are a few additional tips to keep in mind when doing this challenge:

- A negative thought, word, or phrase is anything that causes you to stumble mentally, emotionally, or spiritually. If it doesn't lift you *up*, then it's probably pulling you *down*. If it's bringing you down, write it in the first column.

- Sometimes we blow out of proportion our negative thoughts about ourselves or our circumstances, which causes more anxiety, stress, and discouragement. Rejecting negative thinking is a great tool for putting things back in perspective. The first step to exterminating an ANT is admitting its existence and then forcing yourself to decide on a truer statement about it that helps you regain a more realistic perspective.

- In the "Replace" column, consider that at times a single word will replace the negative thought you've chosen to banish: *grace, peace, beloved, treasured, valuable, worthy, forgiven, hope.* Other times, God may speak a phrase or sentence to your heart: "You're mine," "I've got it," "Release him to Me," or "Trust Me with this." Or the Spirit will prompt your heart with a particular Scripture verse. If so, jot it down and try to memorize it so you can bring it to mind when that ANT pops up again. You might even recall the true words that have been spoken to you by someone who knows and loves you, and you can ask God to help those good thoughts override the negative words or insults spoken against you.

To take this challenge a step further, consider keeping a list—on a notepad, your phone, or somewhere else—of negative thoughts you have to exterminate every day in an effort to begin recognizing patterns of negative thinking. If you don't have time to look up Scripture each time you recognize a negative thought, it's okay. Real change begins when we recognize the thoughts we struggle with and start to form a habit of turning them around and thinking positively instead.

Keeping track on a consistent basis will also help you recognize when you are beginning to think differently and breaking free from the stronghold certain negative thoughts have had over your life. When you notice a change in yourself, get excited!

*Things turn out the best for the people who make
the best of the way things turn out.*

John Wooden

Chapter Six

ROW, ROW, ROW YOUR BOAT

Choosing a Set-Free Mind-Set

*Understanding how our minds are transformed isn't
enough. Every day we need to refuse to let sinking thoughts
enslave us and commit to keep rowing our boats.*

It was a normal day, that is, until God showed up to remind me
how free I truly was.

Years ago, my three young children and I were sitting around
our new Christmas tree, breathing in the fresh scent of pine and
admiring the twinkling lights while the kids made out their holiday
wish lists. Kaitlyn, my daughter, wanted a new doll, prompting
me to tell them all about a fabulous baby doll I had received for
Christmas when I was a little girl. Intrigued with my description,
they squealed, "Oh, Mom, I wish we could have seen her!" My
eyes lit up with excitement, because I had that baby doll tucked
away neatly in the attic, having convinced myself she would one
day become a treasured family heirloom.

I scurried up the steps, opened the attic door, and dug out the box from the other boxes full of forgotten stuff. I took out the doll, dusted her off, straightened her dress, pulled the string on her back that transformed her long red ponytail into a cute short bob, and proudly carried her downstairs to show to my children. I held Baby Crissy up with pride, thrilled to be sharing a piece of my childhood with my own children.

But their reaction did not quite meet my expectations—to put it mildly.

Mouths dropped open, and all three were rendered speechless. Finally, after a few seconds of awkward silence, I said, "What?"

My oldest daughter, Morgan, was the first to speak. With childlike honesty she said, "Mom, that's literally the ugliest baby doll I've ever seen in my entire life. Literally."

Then Kaitlyn said sheepishly, "Yeah, Mommy. She kind of looks like Chuckie" (which shocked me completely because Chuckie was a very scary doll in a horror movie that I had never even allowed them to watch).

My four-year-old son, Michael, was too stunned for words.

Calm down, my hurting heart. We all had a good laugh, then I turned to take Baby Crissy back up to the attic, mumbling under my breath that something was wrong with kids today when they couldn't appreciate awesome toys. But as I was tucking Crissy gently back into her storage box, I caught a glimpse of the doll through their eyes.

All that my children could see was an old, faded doll covered in dirty scuff marks. Crissy was missing every eyelash around her huge, round brown eyes. Seriously, cows might have had smaller eyes than this doll! When my kids looked at Crissy, they saw fuzzy, dull red hair that had been pressed against the side of a box for thirty years, and a dingy, wrinkled dress. They saw a piece of worthless junk. But I saw something completely different. I saw a precious, beloved, and irreplaceable treasure, because I saw beyond Crissy's external imperfections through the lens of my love for her. As I closed the lid and pushed the box back into the corner of the attic, God whispered these thoughts into my spirit:

> *Dear child, remember when you thought all I saw in you was dirty scuff marks and the scars of life? Remember when your heart was so filled with hurt and self-condemning thoughts that you found it hard to believe I loved you or had good plans for you? Remember when you were so perpetually stressed about your circumstances you thought you could never have peace and happiness? Remember when you had a hard time being positive because so much negativity filled your mind? But now you know I see you as My beautiful, beloved child, imperfections and all. Now you enjoy a positive life, despite your circumstances, because you've chosen to let Me help free you from toxic thinking. You invited Me to transform your mind, and as a result, you have changed what you see in your mirror, and in your life.*

My eyes welled up with tears and a smile swept across my face as His powerful whisper brushed through my thoughts. I was suddenly acutely aware of the freedom I now lived in—no longer bound by all those negative thoughts that had chained me to insecurity, self-doubt, fear, sadness, stress, and discouragement. In that sweet moment, I praised God for the freedom He had given me and thanked Him for loving me enough to help me break free from the chains of negativity. Not that I didn't still struggle with my thoughts and emotions from time to time, and I certainly wasn't always a pillar of self-confidence, but I was no longer in bondage to the toxic lies, misconceptions, and negative thoughts that had once poisoned my mind—and my life. I had finally learned the importance of taking all of my negative thoughts captive, regardless if they were about me or my circumstances. This helped me focus on being optimistic instead of pessimistic more often than not.

Every time I did what God had taught me to do—taking my thoughts captive by noticing, rejecting, and replacing negative ones—I grew in freedom and joy.

Where the Enemy Hides

Joyce Meyer once said, "As long as the enemy can hide in our soul, he will always have a certain amount of control over us. But when God exposes him, we are on our way to freedom, *if* we will put ourselves in God's hands and permit Him to do quickly what He desires to do."[1] The key word here is *if*. *If* we continue to deny that we struggle with negativity, persist in blaming people and circumstances for our sour attitudes or outlooks, and keep on failing to believe that we can ever change, we will remain bound to toxic, pessimistic thinking. But *if* we choose to admit our need for change and ask God to expose how and where the enemy lurks and how his tactics are damaging our lives, we are on our way to true freedom and inner peace.

Friend, if you are now recognizing that toxic thinking is something you have struggled with, maybe more than you ever even realized, and you want to experience life-changing freedom and unshakable peace, you can choose to ask God to help you transform and renew your mind right now and God will work with you and in you to make it happen.

Choosing a New Mind-Set

God *can* expose the enemy. He *can* help us find freedom from joy-robbing negativity. And He *can* carry out His will in our lives, but only *if* we invite Him to do so and commit to being a part of the change. Hariet, Marsha, and Rachelle can testify to this truth.

Hariet struggled in college and eventually found herself out of school, unemployed, and not making the best of decisions. She eventually took a job she didn't enjoy and feared she would never get on track with a career she loved. She formed a habit of beating herself up with thoughts of self-doubt and overwhelming regret about poor decisions she had made, and she feared what the future might bring. At one point she became so discouraged and depressed, she even attempted to take her own life. But with the help of family members and friends who encouraged her and prayed for her, Hariet became more aware of what she was choosing to think about. She intentionally and habitually noticed the negative thoughts that made her feel hopeless, upset, and fearful and then replaced them with positive thoughts and encouraging self-talk. She also focused on God's promises in Scripture about her self-worth and read encouraging Christian books that spoke truth into her heart.

Over time, Hariet was able to overcome her sadness and the toxic negativity that had been stumbling blocks in her confidence and her life. She is now back at school, pursuing a degree in education, the career of her dreams. Had she held on to negativity and listened to the lies of the enemy instead of asking God to help her transform and renew her mind, it's likely she'd still be discouraged and *wishing* things were different instead of *making* them different through the power and strength of Christ. She'd most likely still be wondering *if* God could help her transform her mind and rescue her from a life of negativity instead of living in the truth that He *can*.

Hariet did the work to "row her boat."

Marsha spent years harboring negative thoughts and grouchiness toward one of her in-laws who constantly made bad choices that hurt their family and caused disappointment, strife, and distrust. She was completely justified in feeling negative and bitter toward this person, considering all the things he had done, but one day she realized that her negative feelings and thoughts about this person were stealing her joy and affecting her attitude and her other relationships.

She intentionally decided to ask for God to intervene in her heart, while she prayed for this relative's heart as well. She asked God to help her replace her negative thinking about this person with prayers for him, and for the ability and strength to be not only more positive but also more forgiving. Although she still struggles at times with negative feelings when new challenges arise with this person, she no longer feels it is her job to try to change him and has accepted that the only person she can change is herself. As a result, Marsha now experiences more freedom from the anger, frustration, and bitterness that formerly filled her heart and mind. Now she reaps the benefits of not only a more positive attitude but also a more positive life overall.

Marsha did the work to "row her boat."

Because she couldn't find a job elsewhere, Rachelle accepted one that she had never done before in an industry she'd never worked in before. Quickly becoming overwhelmed by the learning curve and figuring out that she didn't like the position, she continually voiced her negativity to a coworker, not realizing it would cause some animosity between them.

After another long and frustrating day, Rachelle found herself in a pit of negativity and noticed how the onslaught of complaints in her mind was affecting her inside and out. She went to God with her feelings and concerns and began praying not for a new job but for a new attitude about the job opportunity God had opened up for her when she was in need. Gradually she realized that when she changed her attitude and replaced her negative thoughts about her job with positive ones, she was able to learn the duties of her position more easily and even develop a friendship with the coworker whom she had been at odds with before.

Rachelle did the work to "row her boat."

Hariet, Marsha, and Rachelle all intentionally chose to change their thought patterns and believe God's promises for joy out of optimism. They refused to allow the enemy to hide in their soul and control their thoughts. They put into practice the habit of noticing, rejecting, and replacing their negative thoughts with God's promises. They pushed forward in God's strength and refused to let negativity keep them from having a positive outlook. They stopped being victims of their circumstances and their thoughts and started enjoying life with positive outlooks.

Great things begin to happen when we choose freedom.

When I accepted who I was in Christ and stopped habitually thinking negative thoughts about myself and my past, my faith grew and God led me to new opportunities to use my pain for His purposes.

When Hariet thought negatively about herself and her future, she couldn't move forward in her career. But when she changed her thinking, she changed her path.

When Marsha thought negatively about the relative who kept making choices that hurt their family, she was always left feeling bitter. But when she chose to pray and think positively about this person— even if and when it was hard to find anything positive about him—her prayer life, her attitude, and her family relationships improved.

When Rachelle chose to look for the positives about her job instead of focusing on the negatives, her happiness, attitude, and work relationships took a turn for the better.

All four of us are experiencing more joy and freedom today, despite our current circumstances, because we chose a set-free mind-set and invited God to renew and transform our thinking.

You too can have a set-free mind-set. Whatever you are struggling with today, God longs for you to be free. You do not have to live another day, or even another moment, enslaved to thoughts that keep you discouraged, stressed, sad, depressed, worried, or hopeless. My prayer is that very soon you will be living in the gift of freedom God offers.

Living in the Freedom Promised You

In Numbers 13:1–31 we find the story of the Israelites being set free from slavery in Egypt. God told Moses in Numbers 13:2 that He was giving them the Promised Land: "Send out men to explore the land of Canaan, the land I am giving to the Israelites." This land was going to be a gift, but the Israelites were so focused on their fears, obstacles, difficult circumstances, and doubt that they were unable to trust in God's promises. They were just outside the Promised Land, but their thoughts steered them in the wrong direction, and the costs were high.

In Numbers 14:1–4 we see where their negative thoughts took them: they became emotionally distraught and exhibited negative actions and behaviors.

> Then the whole community began weeping aloud, and they cried all night. Their voices rose

in a great chorus of protest against Moses and Aaron. "If only we had died in Egypt, or even here in the wilderness!" they complained. "Why is the LORD taking us to this country only to have us die in battle? Our wives and our little ones will be carried off as plunder! Wouldn't it be better for us to return to Egypt?" Then they plotted among themselves, "Let's choose a new leader and go back to Egypt!"

You see, even though the Israelites were physically free, their thoughts were still enslaved to fear, dependency, desperation, pessimism, negativity, and complaining. Despite being positive about their freedom after 430 years in captivity, their negative thinking caused them to feel afraid, hopeless, and powerless. They had a slave mentality instead of a set-free mentality. Although they were physically free, their thinking patterns were still in bondage. Comparing their current situation to the one they'd once had was death dealing. Apparently they were so mentally enslaved to negative thoughts that negative feelings and emotions overwhelmed their hearts and minds, causing them to become physically drained as well. Their negative thoughts and fears had compelled them to be paranoid and afraid and think irrational thoughts while wailing and shouting out of control—all night long. Their thoughts made them feel bad mentally and emotionally, which in turn affected their actions and behaviors, most likely taking a toll on them physically as well.

Dr. Daniel Amen's research reveals that our thoughts can make our minds and bodies feel good or they can make us feel bad, because every cell in the body is affected by every thought we have.[2] Thus when people get emotionally upset about something, they often develop physical symptoms, such as headaches, stomachaches, sweaty palms, a racing heart, flushed faces, crying, distress, or labored breathing. When we think negatively, our bodies react negatively. Surely this is what happened with the Israelites, and maybe you can relate.

But what would it have looked like for the Israelites to have chosen to "row their boat" in the desert? They might have chosen to reject the thought that when they lived in Egypt their lives were better, since it was not true, especially because their experience in Egypt as slaves was actually pretty brutal. They might have expressed confidence in God that, no matter what their circumstances, they trusted Him to be *for* them. But instead, they came completely unglued. Our thoughts directly influence our feelings, which affect our emotions and behaviors and our physical health overall.

I want you to hear that we always have the choice to row our boats. In any circumstance, we can choose to replace a negative mind-set with a positive one. And that choice results in real change in our lives.

Positive Thinking Is a Lifestyle

After the debacle of showing my kids the Crissy doll, I walked back into the kitchen to begin fixing dinner and pondered the change that had occurred in my heart over time. I was overwhelmed with the reality of what God had done in my heart and mind over the years and how, through faith, I had formed a habit of being more aware of what I was thinking, rejecting negative thoughts, and replacing each one with a positive thought and/or something from God's Word. The more time I had spent worshipping God, the less time I had spent worshipping problems and letting them reign over me. When I refused to be enslaved to my negative thoughts, my mind had been slowly transformed.

As I set a pan onto the stove and turned on the burner, I realized that, although it had been a gradual transformation, God had indeed intervened in my heart, mind, and soul when I'd asked Him to. Wave by wave, stroke by stroke, He had helped me take control of my thoughts instead of letting them control and enslave me. He had helped me row my boat, and somewhere along the way, I had chosen to embrace the freedom He had always been offering.

I've learned over the years that positive thinking is a lifestyle, not a onetime accomplishment. It's not something we work on for a while and then become experts on. Mind renewal has to become a daily discipline. The definition of *discipline* is "to train by instruction and exercise; drill; to bring a state of order and obedience by training and control."[3] Transformation happens when we commit to training our minds to think differently by taking control of our thoughts and continuously bringing them into alignment with God's Word. Discipline leads to self-control, which leads to transformation, which eventually leads to freedom.

If you're like me, you may not be a fan of the word *discipline*. We often think of it as being something that causes pain, deprivation, or exhaustion. But trust me—although disciplining our minds might not sound easy at first, knowing it is worth every ounce of effort can motivate us to do it. The discipline required to renew your mind doesn't cause pain, deprivation, or exhaustion but rather leads to joy, fulfillment, peace, and the kind of rest only God can offer. In fact, the discipline of transforming our minds could actually be described as nothing more than exerting willpower, because if we have the will to transform and renew our minds, God has the power.

Galatians 5:1 says, "It is for freedom that Christ has set us free. Stand firm, then, and do not let yourselves be burdened again by a yoke of slavery" (NIV). Negative thinking is a mental burden that enslaves us, and freedom from negative thinking is what God desires for every believer.

When Jesus welcomed the weary to follow Him, He promised that His yoke was easy and His burden was light. You might picture two oxen—you and Christ—harnessed side by side, with Christ bearing the lion's share of the weight of the yoke! I invite you to see, with the eyes of your heart, a similar image as you purpose to row your boat. Every time you do the work of choosing to replace negative thoughts with positive ones, Christ is rowing the boat with you. He is steering you away from slavery and toward freedom, and every ounce of effort exerted will get you closer to the transformation you want to experience.

So keep rowing. I promise you'll get there.

STRATEGIES FOR TRANSFORMING YOUR THINKING

Mind-Transforming Reflections

- When Tracie heard God's whispers following the unexpected comments by her children about her beloved Crissy doll, it was a really big deal. That silly incident signaled the work that He had been doing in her heart and mind as she faithfully rowed the oars and chose to notice, reject, and replace the negative thoughts that had once enslaved her. As you've been working through this book, have you noticed that your thoughts or words, actions or reactions, have changed? Note what's changing inside you, citing specific incidents.

- You've begun to put what you've learned into practice. In what area of your life are you putting the most effort into rowing your boat? Describe what that looks like in your situation. What have you found to be most difficult? What have you discovered to be graciously easy?

- In Numbers 14, the Israelites compare their lives in the desert to the lives they'd lived in Egypt. (They conveniently forgot about the cruel slavery and remembered only the savory meat pots of delicious food.) We can also be tempted to compare our current situations *either* to another period of our lives (that we probably remember being better than it actually was!) or to the lives of others. Which of those two are you most tempted to compare? Ask the Spirit to open your eyes to those places where comparison is draining the life from you. Note each one specifically, and offer it to God.

- Take time to meditate on the One who sits beside you in the boat. As you make life-giving choices to replace your negative thoughts with positive ones, see Christ rowing in tandem with you. Notice how the work becomes lighter with practice. Spend as much time as you wish picturing Christ at your side, helping you with the good work of rowing your boat as you are transformed.

Mind-Renewing Memory Verses

Write out the verses below in your journal, or on your notecards, and commit them to memory.

> For my yoke is easy to bear, and the burden I give you is light. (Matt. 11:30)

> It is for freedom that Christ has set us free. Stand firm, then, and do not let yourselves be burdened again by a yoke of slavery. (Gal. 5:1 NIV)

> For the Lord is the Spirit, and wherever the Spirit of the Lord is, there is freedom. (2 Cor. 3:17)

You say, "I am allowed to do anything"—but not everything is good for you. And even though "I am allowed to do anything," I must not become a slave to anything. (1 Cor. 6:12)

The Spirit who lives in you is greater than the spirit who lives in the world. (1 John 4:4)

Chapter Challenge

The voyage you're on isn't a short one, but it is a very important one. When you ask God to transform your mind, you're choosing to embrace a lifelong journey. But you weren't meant to journey alone.

Is there someone in your life—a neighbor, a sister, a friend— who you think could get fired up about the thought of having a transformed heart, mind, and life? Invite God to bring one or two women to mind who might be blessed to share this journey with you. Your invitation could be as formal as asking a friend to be an accountability partner or it could be as simple as bringing this book to coffee with a Christian sister and asking her to hop into the boat with you. The Christian life was never meant to be a Lone Ranger affair. God delights in gifting us with sisters on the journey so that they can bless us and we can bless them.

Jot down some ideas now and add names as God brings others to mind. Also, set this practical goal: "I'll make a date within the next two weeks to discuss with someone about living life with unsinkable faith and optimism."

God never said the journey would be easy. But he
did say that the arrival would be worthwhile.

Max Lucado

Chapter Seven

INSTRUMENTS NO CREW MEMBER SHOULD BE WITHOUT

Two Tools for the Trip

*Our thoughts can be pitiful or they can be powerful. Scripture
and prayer equip us to navigate through stormy seas.*

I suddenly realized I sounded exactly like her, and she was the last
person I wanted to sound like.

Several years ago I worked in an office with a woman who was
a chronic complainer. Fellow drivers on her morning commute
drove too slowly; work meetings were either too long or irrelevant;
her salary was too low; her boss didn't value her; her cubicle neigh-
bors talked too loudly; her office chair was uncomfortable … on
and on it went.

And her litany of complaints wasn't contained to her work
situation: her family didn't appreciate her; her car was a piece of
junk; her husband never met her needs; her in-laws were intrusive.
She even complained about her grocery store because they had

stopped carrying her favorite brand of detergent. It was not only draining and annoying to listen to this woman day after day, but after a while, her negative attitude became toxic—not just to her, but to me as well.

On one particularly trying day, I was venting some concerns I had to a peer and suddenly became aware I sounded just like her—the chronic complainer. I had been stewing over some things at work that I wished would change. My coworker's naysaying had penetrated my thoughts, affected my attitude, and caused me not only to think but also to act in a less than positive way. Apparently the more I had listened to this woman's pessimism, the more it had infected me.

I stopped my own litany of complaints midsentence, excused myself, and retreated to the privacy of my office. I had been thinking negatively, thus I had become negative. I had failed to protect my mind and spirit (and my ears) from pessimism, and the cost I was paying was not only a complaining attitude but also a lack of joy and fulfillment coupled with an abundance of stress and discontentment. I remembered the truth found in Proverbs 23:7 about how we are what we think and knew I needed to talk to the One who could help me capture those adverse thoughts and turn around my thought patterns.

As I prayed, I realized I had been so caught up in busyness with work and family that I'd put Bible reading and prayer on the back burner. I had not consciously been asking God to help me with my thoughts for quite some time, much less making them captive to the things that would please Him. I couldn't blame anyone else for my own mental outlook, because I was the one who had not protected my own mind. Negativity is highly contagious, and infection can set in if we don't keep our spiritual immune systems healthy.

After quietly closing my office door, I bowed my head and uttered a silent prayer, asking God to forgive me for not only thinking pessimistically but also for spreading the disease of negativity to others. I didn't have the power to change my coworkers or unfavorable job circumstances and knew I needed a paradigm shift in my thinking to have victory over the war for my mind and my happiness, in addition to peace in my job.

I needed tools for the journey.

Addressing the Real Problem

As I sat slumped in my chair, wishing I could start the day over and retract some of the complaints I had verbalized, the Holy Spirit prompted my mind with 2 Corinthians 10:3–5:

> For though we live in the world, we do not wage war as the world does. The weapons we fight with are not the weapons of the world. On the contrary, they have divine power to demolish strongholds. We demolish arguments and every pretension that sets itself up against the knowledge of God, and we take captive every thought to make it obedient to Christ. (NIV)

Paul's words reminded me that I needed to be equipped for the voyage and also that God had already been faithful to equip me with what I needed.

The apostle was speaking to the church of Corinth and the Christians throughout the region. While his letter was written to the Corinthians, his words point to the spiritual battle every Christian faces at one time or another: the battle for dominion over our thoughts. Paul was stating that the Corinthians' enemies were not people who hated him, such as some other teachers of the law, certain Corinthians who had strayed from the teachings of Jesus, or those who had accused Paul of not practicing what he was preaching in an attempt to undermine his credibility as a true apostle. The real enemies they faced were their arguments and their thought processes. In this passage, Paul wanted the Corinthians to know that he knew what the problem was, what the solution was, why it was important to deal with, and how to fight back and experience victory.

When Paul wrote, "We are human, but we don't wage war as humans do" (v. 3), he was letting the Corinthians know he understood what they faced. They wouldn't be warring with wooden clubs, slingshot stones, or metal swords. Paul wanted to encourage the believers that victory was possible and that they were equipped for it.

In the first part of verse 4, he said *the solution* was to choose to fight back with spiritual weapons: "The weapons we fight with are not the weapons of the world" (NIV). Then in the second sentence, "On the contrary, they have divine power to demolish strongholds" (NIV), he explained why they needed to fight back: in order to break down the mental barriers or habitual thought patterns that were causing them to think and act in ungodly ways and preventing them from experiencing the joy of their faith. They didn't have to stay stuck in their mind-sets if they intentionally chose to be free.

Then in verse 5, he wrote, "We demolish arguments and every pretension that sets itself up against the knowledge of God" (NIV). Paul wanted the Corinthians to realize they were being deceived and led astray by the teachings of nonbelievers and the negativity running rampant in their culture. They were in danger of having their minds influenced to see things from the world's perspectives rather than God's.

So he told them *how to fight back:* they needed to take "captive every thought to make it obedient to Christ" (NIV). Some theologians have compared the phrase "taking every thought captive" to the phrase "to take as a prisoner of war," meaning that every thought that goes against what pleases God should be captured, like a prisoner of war, and made to submit to God's authority.[1] Before we can take our negative or ungodly thoughts captive, we have to be aware that they exist. We have to notice them in the shadows of the battlefield, and not let them run free.

Much like the Corinthians, you and I also need to fight back by taking our thoughts captive. The good news is that God has given us the very tools we need to do just that.

Two Powerful Tools

Several years ago, I discovered firsthand what a powerful tool God's Word really is. A friend inspired me to read through the entire Bible, a feat at which I had failed more times than I wanted to admit. I longed to know His story more deeply so I could let it become more of a part of mine, but the thought of actually reading through the entire Bible seemed overwhelming—and frankly, impossible. Yet little did I know that when I finally followed through on that pledge to myself, it would radically transform my faith and help me learn how Scripture truly does transform the mind.

I purchased a chronological Bible and made a commitment to the daily readings. To my delight, this Bible translation read like an amazing novel I couldn't put down and brought Scripture to life in a brand-new way. I passionately dug in to God's Word every morning, and even had a list of five or six questions I answered each day in my journal about what I had read.

At first it was difficult and I didn't always feel spiritually moved by what I read. There were days when it required sheer discipline because my schedule was packed and I was tempted to skip my Bible reading. But after a few months, my reading became such a big part of my faith walk that I couldn't start my day without it.

Hebrews 4:12 says, "For the word of God is alive and powerful. It is sharper than the sharpest two-edged sword, cutting between soul and spirit, between joint and marrow. It exposes our innermost thoughts and desires." Through this Bible reading challenge, God's Word truly came alive to me for the very first time. There were days when a certain passage would jump off the page, speaking directly to a burden I was carrying. On some days I would learn something new and be blown away by it. While on other days, I was moved to tears by what I read, recognizing how His Word was applicable to the very circumstances I was facing and that He was speaking directly to me. Softly, but powerfully.

The more time I spent thinking about who God is and thanking Him for His faithfulness, the less time I spent thinking discouraging thoughts and letting negativity steal my joy. When your mind is filled with the powerful words of God, it becomes easier to capture negative thoughts before they capture you. A mind filled with Scripture and holy promises has little room for negativity.

The second most powerful tool for capturing our thoughts is prayer. Regardless of when we pray, where we pray, or how we pray, heaven listens. Matthew 7:7 says, "Keep on asking, and you will receive what you ask for. Keep on seeking, and you will find. Keep on knocking, and the door will be opened to you." Prayer opens the door for God to transform our minds. If we ask for a transformed and renewed mind, we will receive it.

Prayer is a conversation between us and God and a place where the devil has no say. When we pray, we should choose our words carefully. Charles Capps, who wrote the bestselling book *The Tongue, a Creative Force*, concurred: "The words you speak will either put you over or hold you in bondage. Today many Christian people have been taken captive by their own words. By the prayer of their own mouth they have been set in a position where they cannot receive from God." He also said, "Prayer is your legal right to use faith-filled words to bring God on the scene on your behalf."[2]

Our prayers are words founded on thoughts, so if our thoughts are sinking, our prayer life might be as well. Proverbs 18:21 says, "The tongue can bring death or life." Thoughts released through our words have power. "The Bible says, 'Let us hold fast to the profession [confession] of our faith …' (Hebrews 10:23). It [doesn't] say, 'Hold fast to your prayer.' When you hold fast to your prayer, you're holding fast to the problem, because most of the time you've prayed the problem. Turn loose of the problem and get hold of your confession. Quit praying the problem. And start staying the answer."[3]

If we pray defeat, we will receive defeat. If we just complain to God about our problems and express how everything is hopeless or bleak, we're praying negativity and defeat. But if we talk to God about our problems and challenges, asking expectantly for what we'd like to see happen and trusting in His ways, we are praying victory. When we pray victory, we will receive victory in the exact way God ordains. Consider the following verses, which promise this:

> I tell you, you can pray for anything, and if you believe that you've received it, it will be yours. (Mark 11:24)

> I tell you the truth, if you had faith even as small as a mustard seed, you could say to this mountain, "Move from here to there," and it would move. Nothing would be impossible. (Matt. 17:20)

> You do not have because you do not ask. (James
> 4:2 NASB)

If we desire to be more positive, we can use our words in prayer to ask God to help us renew our minds and our attitudes. Most importantly, we must faithfully expect Him to do so. If we ask, we will receive, says God. We can pray victory, instead of defeat, and not only will our prayer life turn around, but our hearts and minds will too.

Because of our faith, we have the authority to become the captains of our thoughts. These instruments—Scripture and prayer—are the tools every captain needs to safely guide the ship through rocky waters. For the instruments to be useful, of course, we have to use them. Both Scripture and prayer train our minds to catch and redeem our thoughts.

In *Switch on Your Brain*, Dr. Caroline Leaf pointed out that "purposefully catching your thoughts can control the brain's sensory processing, the brain's rewiring, the neurotransmitters, the genetic expression, and cellular activity in a positive or negative direction."[4] In other words, when we use the spiritual tools at our disposal, all of us can learn to capture our thoughts and retrain our minds. It helps to form daily practices like committing to pray continually for God's perspective about our circumstances and putting up Scripture verses around the home. Such habits can change us from the inside out. Thought patterns lead to life patterns, and when our thought patterns are positive, our life patterns will be too.

Using These Instruments

If we seek God's help and create spiritual habits that enable us to make the most of the weapons of God's Word and prayer, we will reap the benefits of better mental and physical health, increased happiness, and a more positive life. Just ask Carolyn, Abbey, Barbara, and Michelle.

When Carolyn was in her seventies, she was diagnosed with stage-4 breast cancer. Yet not once did her friends ever see her act down or negative. When asked how she maintained such a positive attitude and outlook, Carolyn admitted that, although some days were harder than others, she intentionally chose to think positively rather than wallow in self-pity, worry, or negativity. She made the intentional decision to replace negative thoughts with positive thoughts, and her faith helped her develop the spiritual strength to have the perspective of not "Why me?" but "Why not me?" You see, we can think pitiful or we can think powerful. The choice is ours.

Carolyn chose to think powerfully. She used the tools God had offered her to navigate in stormy waters: Scripture and prayer. As she spent time reading her Bible, she would circle the word *joy* wherever it appeared and claimed joy over her life as she underwent various treatments for her cancer. Carolyn clung to God's Word. She also made her prayer life a priority. By virtue of seeking His intervention in controlling her thoughts, she was able to stay positive and joyful even in the midst of extremely hard and, at times, fearful circumstances.

Abbey found similar strength by employing the tools God offered.

As a young first-time mom, Abbey found herself struggling with a negative body image. Although she adored her precious new baby boy, the shape and size of her body had completely changed because of pregnancy and childbirth. For months after her son's birth she felt overwhelmed with negative thoughts and frustrations. It took having a meltdown in a department store dressing room to open her eyes to see that thinking negatively about her body image had become a stronghold and was robbing her of peace and joy in this new season of motherhood. Abbey immediately turned to God in prayer, and He bathed each of her sad, negative thoughts with comforting truths from His Word.

Here are a few of the truths she chose to dwell on:

- I am a new creation in Jesus, because He died on the cross for me. No amount of stretch marks will make me any less valuable to Him (2 Cor. 5:15).
- My body is the house of the Holy Spirit, and the vessel He uses to enable me to walk in the good works He has prepared for me to do (Eph. 2:10).
- It is far more important for me to be clothed in strength and dignity (Prov. 31:25) than that my clothes fit the way I want them to.

Abbey continued to ask God to transform her thinking about her body image, and her perspective about her postpartum body began to change. She learned to accept that the change in shape and appearance that women's bodies go through during and after pregnancy presents them with a unique opportunity to delight in their function rather than despair over their form. She realized that while her stomach wasn't as firm as it was once, it served as proof of God's answers to her and her husband's prayers for a child. Her hips were wider but formed perfectly according to God's design to give birth. Her face seemed fuller, yet it was no less capable of communicating her joy, delight, empathy, and emotion to the little eyes it held captive.[5] The intentional practice of capturing her negative thoughts and replacing them with truths from God's Word transformed her thinking entirely, freed her from negativity, and enabled her to focus on the joy and blessing of her little one rather than critical thoughts about herself.

These are two very different women, of different ages, seasons of life, and circumstances, yet both of them tapped in to the resources God has provided for those who turn to Him. When we change the way we think, we change the way we feel.

Two Moms

It has always been helpful for me, in my walk with Christ, to learn from other women on the journey. I want to share with you the stories of two more women to show you the variety of ways women are navigating stormy seas with grace and freedom as they utilize the powerful tools God offers.

Barbara's teenage daughter struggled with depression and eventually found comfort through self-harming. Barbara began to blame herself for her daughter's issues and constantly entertained thoughts laced with self-condemnation, accusation, and regret, causing her to lose confidence as a mother and even suffer from panic attacks.

She finally got on her knees, and in addition to requesting God heal her daughter, she asked Him to help her transform her thoughts and faith through this trial. She pleaded with God to show her what she needed to do to help a scar-covered teen put down the razor and pick up her Bible for comfort.

So she decided to pick up her own Bible first, and she began to spend more time reading the Word and talking to God in prayer. She took notecards and wrote down verses that encouraged her and comforted her and hung the cards in every room in her home. She made them especially prominent in her bathroom and bedroom, where she often felt most alone with her thoughts. The Psalms became a salve to her wounded, worried heart, specifically Psalm 34:4, "I prayed to the LORD, and he answered me. He freed me from all my fears," which assured her that God heard her prayers, and Psalm 34:7, "For the angel of the LORD is a guard; he surrounds and defends all who fear him," which reminded her that God was watching over her precious daughter and loved her as His own.

Over time, Barbara formed a practice of noticing when negative thoughts threatened to pull her back into fear and discouragement, and of replacing those negative thoughts with something positive from God's promises. She gradually developed a bold confidence in Christ to handle the hard days when they came and was able to maintain a positive outlook even on the most difficult days. Today her daughter is on the way to a full recovery and has learned to turn to Jesus with her frustrations instead of self-harm. Because they have both learned the value of capturing negative thoughts and standing firm in the strength and hope of Christ, their faith has blossomed.

Michelle's story is different but still a vivid example of how choosing optimism changed her life. Her son Cory was diagnosed with cancer when he was just fifteen years old. At first she was overcome with worry and paralyzing fear about what the future might hold, even though her son's attitude was one of faith-filled optimism and peace. She knew she would have to rely on God alone, and asked Him to help her notice and toss out any negative thoughts that crept into her mind. Tapping into the promises in God's Word, she proclaimed to the enemy that she refused to live in a pit of negativity, no matter the outcome. She began to spend time with God first thing every morning and to take note of even the tiniest of blessings.

Although God called Cory home seven months later, Michelle's faith and choice to trust God equipped her spiritually to look for the good that could come from her heartbreaking loss. God held her broken heart in His hands, enabled her to have joy in the midst of heartache, and changed her life. Michelle and her husband, Dale, now run Cory's Project, a ministry to families who find themselves in a battle against pediatric cancer.[6] Although her loss was great and not a day goes by that she doesn't miss her son, Michelle's gains were many. Her commitment to daily control her thoughts resulted in stress reduction, improved physical health, and unsinkable inner peace. Her faith and optimism opened her eyes to see God's divine plan for turning her family's pain into purpose. She would have never imagined or discovered any of this had she succumbed to pessimistic thinking.

Barbara and Michelle both faced battles no mom ever wants to face, but their awareness of capturing their thoughts and submitting them to God, while making His Word and prayer a priority, helped them not only cope with and endure their trials with God's strength and courage but also be victorious in their thinking.

God Provides What We Need

When walking through the difficult situation in my marriage, I was again faced with the choice of who was going to be in control of my thoughts. For months, looming negative thoughts repeatedly forced themselves into my consciousness, challenging me to a duel time and time again. I knew either I could let discouraging, negative thoughts retrain my mind or I could take control of them so they didn't rule over my happiness. So with each negative thought that threatened to pull my mind out to places I didn't want it to go, into choppy seas of sorrow and hopelessness, I would try to capture the thought, submit it to God, and replace it with something hopeful and positive. In order to do that, I had to be fueled by prayer and by the truth of God's Word.

When I felt rejected, I would shift my thoughts to focus on the promise of Scripture: Jesus loved and accepted me. When I felt lonely, I would pray prayers of gratitude for my many friends and family. When I felt afraid, I would bring to mind verses to tackle my emotions and remind myself to trust God's ways as in Psalm 56:3, "But when I am afraid, I will put my trust in You." When worries about the future would threaten to steal my peace, I would prayerfully recall all the times God had protected and provided for me in the past. I spent a lot of time in prayer and relied on God's Word daily to comfort my heart. Some days were really hard. But most days I was able to maintain a positive outlook and try to be thankful for and enjoy all the blessings God had given me, rather than becoming an emotional prisoner of my circumstances.

It wasn't easy for me, nor was it easy for any of these women whose stories I've shared, and it may not come easily for you, but we all have the power to be strengthened by God's good gifts of Scripture and prayer.

Sweet friend, you understand the importance and urgency of taking your thoughts captive to Christ. But what I want you to see and believe is that God has equipped you with what you need to do just that—even if it seems impossible on the surface. As we commit to surrendering our negative thoughts to Christ, God equips us with all we need. The enemy will repeatedly challenge us to duels in the battlefield of the mind, but we've been given powerful spiritual weapons to fight the war.

Prayer and Scripture equip us to learn to be the captain of our own thoughts.

STRATEGIES FOR TRANSFORMING YOUR THINKING

Mind-Transforming Reflections

- Has there been a time in your life when you were nourished deeply by the words of Scripture? What was it about that season—practices, guides, journaling, artistic responses—that made the Bible come alive in your heart and mind? Are there any life-giving practices you can integrate today?

- If there's not been a time when you've been fed by Scripture, consider finding a tool to help. A friend or your pastor or an employee at a Christian bookstore might be able to help you find a devotional guide or themed Bible to lead you deeper into God's Word. God's Word is alive, and nothing beats experiencing it firsthand.

- Has there been a time in your life when prayer felt like a holy encounter with the living God? Record what you remember about that time with God and how you felt after intimately experiencing His presence.

- If there's not been a time in your walk with Christ that you've encountered God in prayer, consider talking to your pastor or a fellow believer. They might be able to suggest different ways of praying to help you connect with God in a way that makes sense for you. Keep in mind that, as in any relationship, communication is necessary and builds intimacy. Ask God to help you begin sensing His presence, and consider purchasing a book or devotional that helps you learn to be more in tune to how He speaks.

Mind-Renewing Memory Verses

Write out the verses below in your journal, or on your notecards, and commit them to memory.

> For the word of God is alive and powerful. It is sharper than the sharpest two-edged sword, cutting between soul and spirit, between joint and marrow. It exposes our innermost thoughts and desires. (Heb. 4:12)

> Put on all of God's armor so that you will be able to stand firm against all strategies of the devil. (Eph. 6:11)

> Keep on asking, and you will receive what you ask for. Keep on seeking, and you will find. Keep on knocking, and the door will be opened to you. (Matt. 7:7)

> Don't bargain with God. Be direct. Ask for what you need. This isn't a cat-and-mouse, hide-and-seek game we're in. (Matt. 7:7 THE MESSAGE)

> I tell you, you can pray for anything, and if you
> believe that you've received it, it will be yours.
> (Mark 11:24)

Chapter Challenge

If you have never read through the Bible or made Bible reading a priority, don't feel guilty about it, but also don't procrastinate on making a change! Sometimes the hardest part of studying the Bible and meditating on it is simply getting started. Commit today to begin making God's Word a priority in your daily routine, and ask Him to breathe life into the verses you read. While reading, if your eyes divert back to one verse over and over, that may be God speaking to you. If a verse seems to be completely relevant to a situation you are facing, that may be God speaking to you. If a story brings you to tears, that may be God speaking to you. There will be days when you may feel you haven't heard anything from Him or felt any spiritually moving emotions. But trust that God is still close by, and when He is ready to speak something of significance into your life, He will. The key to hearing God speak through His Word is reading His Word.

Below are six questions you can use during your quiet time in God's Word to help you be engaged and in tune with what you are reading and to prompt you to be aware of His voice. Consider typing these questions on a piece of a paper, leaving room for answers and thoughts, and making multiple copies to use throughout the year. Place these pages in a three-ring binder, or you can write the questions out in your journal each day instead.

1. Is there a promise to believe in this passage?
2. Is there a sin to avoid?
3. What new thing did I learn about God?
4. How can I practically apply this scripture in my life right now?
5. Does this scripture speak to a certain circumstance or problem I am facing?
6. How do I feel led to pray about what I've read?

(Visit Tracie's blog at www.traciemiles.com to purchase a Daily Bible Reading Journal, which has these six questions prewritten for you and space allowed for your answers. This journal can be used as a digital online journal where you can input your thoughts, or you can print a hard copy version at home.)

A pessimist sees the difficulty in every opportunity; an optimist sees the opportunity in every difficulty.

Winston S. Churchill

Chapter Eight

MAYDAY, MAYDAY!

Let Go of Despair and Grab Hold of Hope

Letting go of what weighs us down mentally, emotionally, and spiritually releases negativity from our hearts and minds. Hearts anchored in God don't sink.

A man was walking through a circus tent and passed a cluster of huge, powerful elephants. He noticed that only a small rope tied to one leg of each animal and attached to a pole was all that was holding them captive. It was obvious creatures of their size and strength could easily break free from their bondage any time they wanted to, but for some reason, they never tried to escape.

The man's curiosity was piqued, prompting him to walk over to the trainer and ask why the elephants stood there passively, with no attempt to get away.

"Well you see, sir," the trainer said to the man, "when the elephants were very young and much smaller, they were tied to a pole with the same size rope, and at such a young age and not much strength, they are unable to break free. As they grew up, their spirits were broken and they became conditioned to believe they could *never* break free. They have grown to accept the belief that the rope still binds them to the pole, so they don't even try to escape."

In the minds of those elephants, that thin rope and pole were as binding and powerful as a large metal chain attached to an anchor sunk into the bottom of the ocean. They believed they were captive; therefore, they were. That false belief altered their lives and kept them from freedom.

We're no different. When we look at our circumstances and feel frustrated or hopeless, and accept the belief we can never be happy or genuinely enjoy life unless or until they change, we're anchored to our negativity. When we look at our past mistakes or failures and accept the belief we are not worthy of God's forgiveness, mercies, and love, we're anchored in lies. When we look at our flaws and imperfections and accept the belief that we can't measure up to the expectations of those around us, or the expectations we've set for ourselves, we're anchored in disappointment and hopelessness. When we rehearse the critical words or uncaring actions of others in our minds day after day, year after year, decade after decade, we're anchored in blame. When we convince ourselves we are the way we are and the way we've always been, and come to believe we can never change—much less break free from a mind-set of negativity and feel happy—then we stay anchored in the pit of bondage.

The result of believing all these false beliefs? Captivity.

As we've seen, it is always our choice whether we allow a lie from the enemy to become a life-altering false belief in our minds.

When we allow it, we're stuck. Tied to a stake, anchored in the bay. Graciously, God wants to set us free. Lamentations 3:23 says, "Great is his faithfulness; his mercies begin afresh each morning." God's craftsmanship—God's work in the world and work in our lives—is always ongoing. We cannot always change our circumstances and we can never change our past, but we can always change who we will be in the future when we release the weight that's holding us down.

Letting Go of Negativity

When Gaye and her husband practiced one brave act, they were released from their chains. After getting involved with the wrong crowd, their son went through a long season of poor decisions as a teenager, which eventually led to excessive drug and alcohol use. Gaye and her husband prayed faithfully for years and took their son to multiple Christian counselors, convinced they should be able to fix the problem as his parents. Gaye became bound to the lie that she should be ashamed of their son's struggle and lived in fear of exposure and judgment from others. As a result, she and her husband kept all their sadness and fear to themselves, and at their highest point of frustration, they expressed a sentiment to each other, which was dripping with anguish: "We have lost our son."

Because it seemed that nothing they tried was helping to solve their son's problems, Gaye and her husband became bound to the falsehood that all was hopeless. With each passing month, they found themselves sinking deeper and deeper into despair, tied to the anchor of hopelessness. Then one day they decided to let go of their pessimistic thinking and anchor their hearts in God instead. They took a leap of faith and shared their struggle with other Christian parents at church. With that intentional act, they let go of the despair that had been pulling them under and grabbed hold of the One who could rescue them—God.

To their surprise, they were overwhelmed with love and concern. Many other parents confessed that they had been going through a similar struggle. Through prayer and fellowship, Gaye and her husband were gradually able to let go of their discouraging thoughts and let God take over. In doing so, they were set free from fear, shame, and helplessness. Their faith and positive frame of mind were instrumental in their transformation, as well as their son's. Today he is a clean, sober, and vibrant Christian.

The key to changing our mind-set lies in learning to let go of what weighs us down mentally, emotionally, and spiritually. We must refuse to latch on to negative thoughts that cause us to sink and instead grab hold of hope.

Grabbing Hold of the Anchor of Hope

In November 2007, Alan Ryden, a commercial fisherman in Alaska, embarked on a month-long trip at sea in his forty-two-foot vessel called *Pacific Lady*. A violent storm brewed, and despite his fishing and boating expertise, the boat capsized under the strength of incredible winds and waves up to thirty feet high. Quick thinking enabled him to hurriedly put on his survival suit and fleece jacket, while sending out several Mayday calls to the Coast Guard. It was a hard-fought struggle to release the life raft into the sea, and although Alan was being tossed about like a play toy in the frigid waves, he felt a sense of relief to be free from the capsizing boat.

Alan knew the emergency radio beacon would send out a locating signal as soon as the boat sank to below ten feet, but he had no idea how long it would take for that to occur and was unsure if his Mayday calls had even been heard. As he sat in the raft alone, shivering and afraid, he struggled with negative thoughts as his mind went to places where deep discouragement and hopelessness brewed as fiercely as the storm that surrounded him. Certain he would die a slow death, Alan ruminated:

> *I wonder if my life insurance will pay off, and will it be enough for Amy and the boys?*

Alan's thoughts were pulling him under more than the waves pounding against his small raft—until the life-altering moment when he decided to take control of them. He committed to himself to think only positive inward thoughts from that moment forward, even though his external situation seemed to be worsening.

> *I am going to see a Coast Guard helicopter coming over the horizon before dark, and I'll be in the steam room on the Coast Guard base in an hour, and on my couch with a cup of tea.*

He brought to mind scriptures and spoke God's Word aloud and then decided to focus on things of which he could be thankful for, even in the middle of this life-threatening circumstance.

> *Well, at least I am in a survival suit. My suit does have a top-of-the-line strobe light attached ... At least I am in some kind of raft, and at least I got that fleece jacket on before I pulled the suit on ... I am strong, a good swimmer, and have no fear of the water.*
>
> *I shall live and not die! (Ps. 118:17).*

He even surmised that exerting physical energy to keep climbing back on the raft was God's way of keeping him warm enough to survive. That thought made him laugh and feel grateful.

But as darkness set in, despite his efforts to think and speak positively, his spiritual battle intensified and the battle for control of his mind grew fiercer. Alan found himself entertaining thoughts of hopelessness, and he became aware that with every pessimistic thought, he could feel himself getting colder. So instead of succumbing to negative thoughts, he chose to shift his thinking and grab hold of hope. He wrote this about the defining moment when he chose to think positive instead of negative thoughts: "There was definitely a grace from God to keep my mind on 'the life' in the situation, but the battle to stay there versus giving up or even considering the impossibility of hope in this situation was very real. I had to fight for every inch in my thoughts with my words."[1] He not only thought positively, he spoke positively as well, even though the only person who could hear him was God.

Ten long hours later, when Alan heard the sound of a four-engine plane roaring above him, he knew he had been located and would soon be rescued. Eventually a Coast Guard boat picked him up.

Although Alan was physically rescued from the stormy waters, God had rescued Him in his thoughts long before that occurred. He experienced a spiritual rescue the moment he grabbed on to hope. In the midst of the storm, he anchored himself in God and embraced positive thoughts, which helped him stay buoyant.

After his rescue, Alan summed up this battle of the mind perfectly when he said, "We are in a state of being actively deceived if we stay focused on our weakness and walk in anything less than who we are. We will walk in what we confess and focus on our own thoughts. It is a heated battle for our minds and tongues only because the enemy is well aware of what we can do if we actually believe the Word."[2]

In Lamentations 3, we see a similar story of hope and victory over thoughts. In the first fifty-three verses, the author, who researchers believe to be the prophet Jeremiah, expressed with great angst and description the heartache and fears he was struggling with over the recent destruction of Jerusalem and the overall presence of evil and suffering in the world. His thoughts were pulling him under like a heavy anchor, causing him to feel like he was drowning.

> The water rose over my head,
>   and I cried out, "This is the end!"
>
> But I called on your name, LORD,
>   from deep within the pit.
> You heard me when I cried, "Listen to my
>   pleading!
>   Hear my cry for help!"
> Yes, you came when I called;
>   you told me, "Do not fear." (Lam. 3:54–57)

The term *lamenting* means to mourn or to feel or express grief, and sums up the theme of the book of Lamentations. In the original book of Hebrew, Lamentations was called "*ekah,*" which can be translated as "Alas!" or "How?"—both of which are terms that imply great shock and troubled emotions and give us a glimpse into the types of thoughts plaguing the prophet's mind.[3] Jeremiah felt like he was sinking, as if circumstances were making it impossible for him to keep his head above water. Yet there was no literal water; he was sinking in negativity and discouragement.

As you are aware from the personal experiences I've shared with you so far, I've certainly found myself in the same boat as Jeremiah before, feeling as if I were drowning in my thoughts, and I imagine you have too. Another such example was when my daughter experienced heartbreaking bullying and rejection at school. I recall how my feelings of helplessness to fix the situation, mend her heart, and rebuild her self-confidence made me feel like I was sinking. I've also watched my sister struggle with a debilitating illness for over twenty years and often find myself sinking in sadness over her plight, powerless to ease her suffering. Because of these situations and so many others, I've learned one very important thing: any negative thought that goes uncaptured will eventually cause us to sink.

Whether because of a failed marriage or a prodigal child, negative thoughts like regret and worthlessness can cause us to sink. Whether because of a failing financial situation or an unexpected health diagnosis, negative thoughts fueled by overwhelming fears of the unknown can cause us to sink. Whether we find ourselves physically homeless or facing the heavy quietness of a new empty nest, negative thoughts of loneliness and sadness can cause us to sink.

In the passage below, we see that Jeremiah chose to listen to God's prompting to trust Him and not be fearful. Despite all of his hardships and grief, he chose to put his hope in God.

> I will never forget this awful time,
>   as I grieve over my loss.
> Yet I still dare to hope
>   when I remember this:
>
> The faithful love of the LORD never ends!
> His mercies never cease.

> Great is his faithfulness;
>> his mercies begin afresh each morning.
> I say to myself, "The LORD is my inheritance;
>> therefore, I will hope in him!"
>
> The LORD is good to those who depend on him,
>> to those who search for him.
>> (Lam. 3:20–25)

The prophet professed with his words his hope in God's faithfulness and intentionally shifted his thinking. He chose to think positively and anchored his hope in God alone. Envision Jeremiah grabbing hold of this hope. I can almost see the shackles falling from Jeremiah's body. He released his grip on the anchor of negativity and chose to grab hold of God instead. He sought rescue in God, and was rescued.

Like him, you and I can't *forget* our difficult circumstances or the hardships of our past, but we can choose to shift our thinking about them. We can decide to let God's hope be the anchor for our souls. Diane is a beautiful example of someone who did just that.

Diane's Story

For two years, Diane lived with a man who was an emotionally and physically abusive alcoholic. She finally escaped from the relationship and went to live in a shelter for abused women, but the abuse had rendered her a broken, battered mess, inside and out. Her physical wounds healed, but the invisible wounds from the verbal and emotional abuse lingered, leaving her feeling hurt, resentful, and worthless. She struggled with strong feelings of hatred toward this man who had broken her heart and her spirit. As a result, she became bitter toward all men, even her own brothers. She was afraid to get close to or trust anyone, even God.

But after six weeks of intense counseling with godly mentors and teachers in the shelter, Diane moved in with loving family members and slowly began to heal, as God helped her put the pieces of her heart and her life back together. She began reading God's Word and spending a lot of time in prayer.

She had been attending church for several months when she heard a powerful sermon about forgiveness that stirred her soul. She practically ran to the altar when the message was over, asking the pastor to pray that her heart would soften toward her abuser and that God would give her the strength and ability to truly forgive. Although it didn't happen instantaneously, Diane's heart did soften over time.

She began to look forward to each new day instead of dreading it. She was excited to be with new friends, learned to trust people again, and allowed herself to believe there were good Christian men in this world. One of those men helped her embrace her value in Christ, and Diane is now happily married to him! When she forgave the unforgivable, she broke free of the bondage of hatred and stopped the poison of negativity that had been coursing through her veins. When she made the decision to let go of her negative strongholds and anchor her heart on God instead, His peace took up residence in her heart and happiness filled her days.

Diane underwent a paradigm shift, and so must we.

Undergoing a Paradigm Shift

A paradigm shift takes place when the usual way of thinking is replaced by something different. It's a fundamental change in approach or assumptions about a certain subject.[4] Simply put, it's a critical change from one way of thinking to another. In Romans 12:2, the apostle Paul called all believers to allow God to help them make a paradigm shift: "Let God transform you into a new person by changing the way you think." I like how *The Message* puts it:

> So here's what I want you to do, God helping you: Take your everyday, ordinary life … and place it before God as an offering. Embracing what God does for you is the best thing you can do for him … You'll be changed from the inside out.

We experience a paradigm shift when we release our everyday lives and thoughts. Doing so frees us up to embrace what God has done for us and what He longs to do in us.

It's how we're transformed.

Release negativity. Embrace hope.

What if we received whatever God allowed in our lives—good or bad—with a positive attitude and trusted that He is in control and working for our good behind the scenes? What if we began to evaluate what we think about and controlled our perspective, trying to keep in line with God's perspective rather than letting our thoughts control us and sink us in negativity and discouragement? What if we consciously tried to take our thoughts captive each day?

When we ask God to free us from the thoughts that keep us anchored to negativity and discouragement, He partners with us and willingly cuts the ropes that bind. God is holding out the anchor of hope that will keep you safe in the midst of the storms of life. You only need to grab hold.

STRATEGIES FOR TRANSFORMING YOUR THINKING

Mind-Transforming Reflections

- When we walk past hulking elephants tethered by thin ropes, it's obvious that what's binding them is without any real power. Others may think the same when they notice what weighs us down! Throughout this book you've considered various lies and negative thoughts that have kept you stuck. If you could identify the most powerful anchor weighing you down today, what would it be? As you pray, visualize that anchor as being as flimsy as a thin worn rope. Invite God to set you free.

- When Gaye and her husband shared their struggles at church, they experienced freedom. That one brave, honest act was what it took to let go of their anchor and grab hold of the rescue God had in store for them. Is there one brave, honest act to which God is calling you today? What might you need to let go of so you'll be free to anchor your heart in God? As you pray, invite God to prompt your heart if He is calling you to take action on what you believe about freedom.

- Lost at sea, at risk of hypothermia, Alan Ryden was in a desperate situation. And yet he reached for the hope and truth God offered. What has been the most negative circumstance you've experienced that weighed you down? What rescue did God provide? If you can't identify one, prayerfully imagine what God may have offered that you missed. What is it? How might you have accessed it?

• When God convicted Diane's heart that she needed to forgive, she responded with joyful obedience and was set free. Is there someone in your life who God is inviting you to forgive? Converse with God in your journal about who you might need to forgive. Remember that forgiveness is so we can experience freedom, regardless if the other person deserves it. Letting go of what weighs us down frees our hearts to grab hold of Who will raise us up. This is a precious opportunity to find freedom!

Mind-Renewing Memory Verses

Write out the verses below in your journal, or on your notecards, and commit them to memory.

> The faithful love of the LORD never ends!
>   His mercies never cease.
> Great is his faithfulness;
>   his mercies begin afresh each morning.
>   (Lam. 3:22–23)

> So if the Son sets you free, you will be free indeed.
> (John 8:36 NIV)

"Lᴏʀᴅ, help!" they cried in their trouble,
and he saved them from their distress.
(Ps. 107:28)

You came to my rescue, Lord, and saved my life.
(Lam. 3:58 ɢɴᴛ)

We have this hope as an anchor for our lives, safe
and secure. (Heb. 6:19 ʜᴄsʙ)

Chapter Challenge

In the middle of a piece of paper, draw a horizontal line and a stick figure of you on the surface of the water and starting to sink in the ocean. At the bottom of the picture, draw an anchor stuck in the sand floor, and then draw a line tethering the anchor to your foot. On the surface of the water, draw a life preserver (as a symbol of hope) and then draw a line tethering the life preserver to your hand. There you are in the middle: caught between sinking and rescue!

On the line tied to the anchor, write down those thoughts, feelings, or circumstances that make you feel as if you're drowning. Then on the rope tethering you to a life preserver, write the words *hope, joy, peace, optimism*, and *freedom*. You could also write down Scripture verse references that remind you of those holy gifts. Then look at your picture. Let it serve as a visual of what is causing you to sink, as well as the promise of rescue that is within your reach.

Would you rather stay tied to the anchor of negativity, or grab hold of hope and experience new life? Life with joy, optimism, and hope—not because anything changed on the outside, but because you allowed God to change you on the inside.

Say a prayer and ask God to free you from the ties that bind. The circumstances that steal your joy and peace. The memories that haunt you. The failures that sting you. The words and actions that wounded your heart. Ask for spiritual courage, strength, and perseverance to embrace the life preserver He is offering you. Thank Him for the tools He has used to rescue you from negativity, such as a certain passage of Scripture, an answered prayer, a friend or accountability partner, or maybe even this book. Seek to see and feel His holy presence. Ask for strength and courage to keep hanging on to Him as your anchor in life.

Keep your face to the sunshine and you cannot see a shadow.

Helen Keller

Chapter Nine

STAY ALERT AND BE PREPARED!

Navigating the Whirlpools on the Voyage

If you think the voyage will be all smooth sailing,
think again. When we're the captains of our thoughts,
we can learn to avoid the whirlpools.

Just a few years ago I was invited to speak at a large national women's conference. As I sat in the lobby waiting for my transportation to arrive, some of the other conference speakers congregated there as well. I eyed them from across the room, and out of nowhere, I found myself thinking about how confident they appeared, how pretty they were, and how professional they were dressed. I began wondering whether the other speakers were more experienced than I was, if their messages would be more encouraging than mine, if they were more powerful speakers, if they were more successful in their ministries, if the attendees would like them better, on and on it went. As I compared myself to these women, my mind was filled with thoughts of insecurity and inferiority. Before I knew it, I felt like I was the ugly stepsister at the ball, wondering why in the world I had been asked to speak at this conference. And why in the world I had agreed.

Without warning, the devil had swooped in and filled my head with anxious thoughts that led to negative emotions. I sensed my heart beginning to race and noticed I was sinking, as waves of self-doubt washed over me.

Fortunately, because this wasn't the first time I had fallen headfirst into a whirlpool of paralyzing thinking, God instantly convicted me. I noticed my negative thoughts, recognized they were pulling me under, and captured and rejected them in prayer. I began to control my thinking instead of letting my thoughts drown my confidence and enthusiasm, and soon I realized nothing I was telling myself was from God.

I silently recited Psalm 139:14, "Thank you for making me so wonderfully complex! Your workmanship is marvelous—how well I know it," and Ephesians 2:10, "For we are God's master-piece. He has created us anew in Christ Jesus, so we can do the good things he planned for us long ago." Then Proverbs 4:23 came to mind, "Be careful how you think; your life is shaped by your thoughts" (GNT). I was so thankful I had tucked these verses into my memory and could call on them to replace the negative thoughts that were threatening to suck me into their vortex. Right then and there, I had a chat with little ol' me and reassured myself that if God had called me to speak at this specific event, then I was equipped and capable in His strength and wisdom, not my own, and I needed to trust in His plan and purpose for the weekend.

You see, when the battle began in my mind that morning, I recognized it as a spiritual attack and immediately picked up my God-tools to fight back. I knew I had the power to control my own thoughts, which would drive my entire attitude and outlook. Thankfully I recognized the enemy was trying to submerge me in a whirlpool of negativity, and I tapped into that power instead of allowing my thoughts to pull me under.

Had I tied myself to the anchor of negative thinking that morning instead of being anchored in hope, my whole day could have been ruined and the enemy could have prevented me from reaching others for Christ. Instead, I implemented the three steps outlined in this book—noticing, rejecting, and replacing negative thoughts—and was able to avoid letting my thoughts pull me under. Go me! (Smiles.)

The Struggle Is Real

A critical key to avoiding whirlpools in our thinking is to be aware that they actually exist.

As believers, we must stay alert for spiritual attacks that happen in our thought life and always be spiritually prepped for battle against the enemy at any given time. Regardless of what person, circumstance, or adversity is weighing on our minds, we can be assured that each temptation toward discouragement is a call to battle.

More frequently than not, spiritual warfare happens so slowly and quietly that we fail to recognize the battle has begun. In fact, way too many times in my own life, when it seemed nothing was going right and wave after wave of problems and discouragement kept pounding against my mind, I remember thinking either I had the worst luck in the world or maybe God just wasn't paying attention or hearing my prayers. But then through prayer and Scripture, He would gently remind me there was a battle going on for my peace of mind, optimism, and happiness. When we realize we're under attack and put on the armor of God, only then can we fight for our happiness. When we start fighting back in the battlefield of the mind, victories will result instead of defeat.

When my friend Julie was dealing with the reality of her divorce becoming final—a divorce she didn't want because she still loved her husband—her dreams for her future died along with her marriage. She tied her lost hopes and dreams to the anchor of sadness and was pulled deeper and deeper into a powerful, swirling whirlpool of darkness and depression.

However, one day during a moving worship service, she heard God speak in her spirit, saying, "Julie, let it all go."

She immediately thought, *But I don't want to.*

But God opened her eyes to see that she had been hanging on to the misconception that she had lost everything by virtue of her marriage ending. Her thoughts were sinking her more than her circumstances.

Julie went and knelt before a cross in the sanctuary, stretched out her arms toward it, and prayed for God to take away the stronghold of sorrow and despair that were consuming her every thought. As she lowered her arms and stood, she felt all those lost dreams, ideals, and hopes roll off her heart and onto the feet of Jesus. Weeping, she realized that they had been causing her to sink. After that experience, she reached out for her life preserver, and God was there to pull her back up. She began to cling to His promises for a hope and a future. She chose to stand firm in her faith, pick up her God-tools, and fight back against the enemy's attacks. She reclaimed her thoughts, and as a result, she reclaimed her life.

What God did for Julie—freeing her from the weight of negativity and hopelessness—He wants to do for all of His children. Sometimes it just takes realizing we need to be rescued so that a holy rescue can take place. When we reclaim our thoughts, we can reclaim our lives.

If we ignore the reality of spiritual warfare in our lives, we won't be alert to the enemy's attacks on our thoughts—which is exactly what he wants because that makes us easy prey. First Peter 5:8 says, "Stay alert! Watch out for your great enemy, the devil. He prowls around like a roaring lion, looking for someone to devour."

If we aren't mentally and spiritually prepared for battle, it is unlikely we will win. We're most vulnerable to Satan's attacks when we're feeling sad, insecure, angry, afraid, discouraged, and hopeless, because when we neglect to anchor our minds in Christ, those emotions can easily pull us under. When we stay alert to the reality that there really is an enemy on the prowl ready to pounce at any moment, and when we equip ourselves to stand firm and fight back, God can transform our thinking and keep us afloat.

The struggle is real and the deceiver is tricky. It's easy to overlook the enemy's tactics because they're woven into the thoughts and emotions of normal experiences. He uses different strategies to tempt us into getting sucked into a whirlpool of negativity.

The devil is opposed to us having a mind transformed and renewed by Christ, and he will do whatever it takes to keep us from reaching for victory. So let's take a look at ten of these dangerous temptations, or whirlpools, in the hopes that you will stay alert and won't allow the devil to suck you in.

Stay on the Lookout for ...

Comparison

On that early morning before my conference, when I noticed my thoughts were sinking, I was tempted to magnify my perceived shortcomings while minimizing the possible shortcomings of others. I felt I wasn't worthy and that the other speakers most likely were. I stepped right into the comparison trap and got caught, based on my assumptions alone. In our thoughts, the enemy will try to lure us into the trap of comparison, and the result will always be a lack of confidence and self-esteem. Without holy confidence in who we are and Whose we are, we are less likely to let our faith drive our thoughts and actions.

"Awfulizing"

My daughter was working at a summer camp when a seven-year-old boy walked up to her with slumped shoulders and a melancholy look on his face and said, "I have no luck at all. My life is falling apart."

Taken aback by the boy's comment, Morgan asked what he meant. He replied with his bottom lip poked out, "My brother hates me. He doesn't ever want to be around me or hang out with me."

Assuming the brother was a middle schooler or teenager, she asked how old he was, to which the boy responded, "One and a half years old." She chuckled and gave the boy a hug, assuring him that his brother was just a baby and did love him, and that his life was definitely not falling apart.

This sweet boy did what we are often tempted to do at times—"awfulize" a situation with "all or nothing" thinking. If people don't respond in a way we feel they should, we assume they are against us. We convince ourselves that if some things aren't good, nothing is good. If someone doesn't like us, nobody likes us. If a circumstance is hard, then our whole lives are hard. If we fail at doing one thing, we are a failure overall. If we make a mistake in life, then we are a mistake. Our thoughts and emotions cause us to lose our perspective. Keeping things in perspective is important, because our thoughts, feelings, and behaviors are based on how we see and interpret the things going on in our lives.

Exaggerating

All too often we tend to exaggerate our problems, and rather than stay focused on the one thing we are worried about, we allow it to bleed into our thoughts about everything. We use phrases like "I'm never going to get a job," "Nobody cares about me or will ever love me," "I'm always going to be overweight," "I'll forever be stuck with this problem," "It's been a bad day so it's obviously going to be a bad week," and "I can never change." Or even "My life is over since my marriage is over." Such statements are usually way out of proportion to reality and not true in the least, yet they are all too common. Through the Holy Spirit within us, we can learn to recognize these telling words in our speech: *always, never,* and *forever.* Learning to be aware when our minds are taking a wrong turn about something helps us avoid feeling hopeless about our situations.

Complaining

Remember my former coworker who complained incessantly? She struggled with the ability to filter out bad thoughts and concentrate on good thoughts. Rather than focusing on the fact that she had a good-paying job in a beautiful office, with a stable company and great benefits, in addition to a family who loved her, she obsessed over trivial annoyances. She could never see the good, because every day she stayed laser focused on the not-so-good.

When we constantly look for the negatives in something, we will most always be successful in finding them. When we fill our minds with negative thoughts, we are essentially filtering out the positive ones, which causes us to overlook the small blessings tucked into everyday living. We form a habit of complaining that robs us of joy and also threatens to infect those around us with negativity. If we want to live life seeing the roses instead of the thorns, it's imperative to be aware of how we are filtering our thoughts.

Blaming

Anytime we feel unhappy or discontent, we are often tempted to blame something or someone. A coworker is tempted to blame her peers for her disgruntled attitude because they're not pulling their load. A wife is tempted to blame her husband because his choices destroyed a marriage. A friend is tempted to blame an ex-friend because she broke her trust. A mom is tempted to blame her kids because they keep misbehaving. A woman is tempted to blame her father for her low self-esteem because he never showed her love and approval. The more we latch on to blaming someone else for how we feel, the more we allow that person to have control over our thoughts and our joy. Blaming often chains us to unforgiveness, which infects our minds with negativity and becomes a poison in our hearts. Although the reasons for blaming someone else for our unhappiness may feel justified, and may even be justified, doing so only steals our own joy and peace. We can choose to blame, or we can choose to forgive, and that choice is the determining factor between negativity and unhappiness, optimistic thinking and true joy.

Self-Condemnation

When one of my children went through a season of making poor choices, I constantly told myself I must be a terrible mother. I was certain that had I been a better parent, a better person, or a better Christian, my children wouldn't have made certain mistakes. Satan tempted me to latch on to faulty emotional reasoning, and I got sucked into a whirlpool of negativity because I mistook my feelings for facts. As a result, I felt less confident in my parenting and often wondered if I was cut out for the job.

If you've ever raised a child, I'm sure you can relate. But if God calls us to be the parent or guardian of a child, then He has predetermined we are the best person for the job. We will never be perfect parents, but if we rely on God, who is the perfect parent, we will be equipped to rear our kids the best we can and trust He holds their lives in His hands. Just as our enemy wants us to condemn ourselves if our kids don't always walk the straight and narrow, he also wants us to feel condemned for our imperfections and struggles, both past and present. He wants us to hold on to the anchors of shame and regret in order to prevent us from living with a positive outlook. When we make the choice to listen only to God's voice and not the enemy's, optimism has a much better chance of taking root in our hearts and minds.

Overthinking

When one of my daughters began struggling with migraine head-aches in middle school, my over-researching of her symptoms on the Internet led me to think catastrophic thoughts about what else might be wrong with her. I allowed my mind to entertain the worst-case scenarios, which were far worse than the actual issue. I catastrophized the problem in my mind and let my thoughts run rampant with worry. Unnecessary stress and negative thinking ensued, which affected my ability to think rationally and caused me to lose sleep with worry. The more we think about a problem, the bigger it always becomes in our minds. When we worry, we're focused on our problems, but when we pray, we're focused on our God, who can handle them. We should do whatever we can do, but not worry about whatever we cannot do. Casting our cares on God frees us from the trap of overthinking.

Negative Influences

If we regularly listen to gossip or negative talk, it will begin to affect our thoughts. As we've seen, negativity is highly contagious, and the more we are around negative people, the more apt we are to think like them. Likewise, if we fill our minds with negative things that are surely not pleasing to God, from television, movies, videos, or social media, the harder it becomes to take and keep our thoughts captive to Christ. All temptations to be negative start with what we see and what we hear. Whatever goes in will eventually come out.

Victim Mentality

Most of us have experienced difficult situations in our lives where we felt like victims—victims of someone else's actions, victims of our own choices, or victims of circumstances beyond our control. But living with a victim mentality traps us in a negative mental state of mind and makes us feel helpless and hopeless. It causes us to live in a perpetual pity party, maybe stuck in the past, chained to a pessimistic and discouraged attitude. If the enemy can keep us tied to a victim mind-set, we eventually succumb to the bondage and are soon robbed of happiness and peace. Remember, we can think pitiful, or we can think powerful.

All-Is-Lost Mind-Set

My friend Julie's biggest challenge regarding her divorce was not only the breakup of her marriage but also the death of her dreams. She had always dreamed of having a husband, two kids, and a dog, along with a white picket fence and a happily-ever-after life full of weddings, grandchildren, family holidays, and growing old together. But when her marriage died, those dreams died too. This led her to believe she'd lost everything.

No matter the circumstances that have caused us to feel a great loss, when life suddenly changes, it's easy to begin drowning in our feelings and fears and even experience debilitating depression. When we hold on to a mind-set that all is lost and that happiness can never be ours again, all because we experienced something negative or God allowed something to be taken away, we tie ourselves to an anchor of hopelessness, which prevents us from allowing God to fill our hearts with new hopes and dreams.

Staying Afloat and Refusing to Sink

Remember the two mighty tools that God has already equipped you with? Scripture and prayer are God's good gifts to rescue you from any whirlpool of negativity. When we ask God for a total mind makeover and begin to take our thoughts captive, the enemy will surely try to make us stumble. Let that be a sign that change is happening within you! Opposition is affirmation that God is at work in your heart and mind. We can let opposition make us weaker, or we can stand strong in our faith and refuse to sink.

When we stay acutely aware of what tempts us to be discouraged and negative, and immerse ourselves in prayer and Scripture, we can grow stronger mentally, emotionally, and spiritually. With each little step toward optimism, we draw closer to victory. But, oh my goodness, it's a hard battle! Ephesians 6:10–11 says, "God is strong, and he wants you strong. So take everything the Master has set out for you, well-made weapons of the best materials. And put them to use so you will be able to stand up to everything the Devil throws your way" (THE MESSAGE). My friend, the devil will not cease throwing problems our way. That's his job. But it's God's job to stand in the gap and fight for us. Every day we will encounter experiences and feelings that can trip us up. So if we want to have an unsinkable faith, we need to use the spiritual weapons of prayer and God's Word so we can form steadfast habits to reject negative thoughts and replace them with God's truth.

Here are some examples of how we can avoid getting sucked into a whirlpool of negativity when the enemy tempts us.

To avoid falling into the trap of comparison, we can train our minds to notice when that is happening, pause to pray, and ask God to help us fight the temptation to compare. We can replace our negative thoughts with verses like these, which remind us of how valuable we are to Christ and how dearly and unconditionally He loves us.

> I praise you because I am fearfully and
> wonderfully made;
> your works are wonderful,
> I know that full well. (Ps. 139:14 NIV)

> But God showed his great love for us by sending
> Christ to die for us while we were still sinners.
> (Rom. 5:8)

When in the midst of awfulizing our issues or problems, we lose perspective about reality. Instead we can ask God to help us control our thoughts and feelings, and try to see things from His perspective and not our own. This will help us keep our emotions in check.

> In his kindness God called you to share in his
> eternal glory by means of Christ Jesus. So after
> you have suffered a little while, he will restore,
> support, and strengthen you, and he will place
> you on a firm foundation. (1 Pet. 5:10)

When we catch ourselves exaggerating our problems by using terms like *never*, *always*, and *forever*, we can focus our thoughts on verses that remind us that God is in control of our situations and our future. When we trust God, instead of assuming the worst, we open the door for Him to fill us with peace in the midst of less than peaceful circumstances.

> For the word of the LORD holds true,
>   and we can trust everything he does.
> (Ps. 33:4)

Trust in the LORD with all your heart;
do not depend on your own understanding.
(Prov. 3:5)

When we stop focusing on all the bad things and choose to focus on good things instead, we will be more grateful and less likely to complain. Less complaining and more gratefulness always make for a happy heart and mind.

Do everything without complaining and arguing.
(Phil. 2:14)

And whatever you do or say, do it as a representative of the Lord Jesus, giving thanks through him to God the Father. (Col. 3:17)

When we are tempted to blame others for our negative thoughts and feelings, we can ask God to show us the truth and we can use this verse as a weapon:

People may be right in their own eyes,
but the LORD examines their heart.
(Prov. 21:2)

When we are prone to keep a record of our sins and imperfections and to assume we are damaged beyond repair, we can begin seeing ourselves through the eyes of Christ by replacing those thoughts with verses like this:

> Thank you for making me so wonderfully
> complex!
> Your workmanship is marvelous—how well
> I know it. (Ps. 139:14)

We can pray, asking Him to help us learn to love ourselves solely because of who He made us to be. When we feel loved and valued, we act loved and valued and can better show God's love to those around us.

When we find ourselves overthinking our problems, letting fears rule our hearts, and feeding worry with our thoughts, these verses can prep our spirits to receive the peace of God that surpasses all understanding.

> So don't worry about tomorrow, for tomorrow
> will bring its own worries. Today's trouble is
> enough for today. (Matt. 6:34)

> Then you will experience God's peace, which
> exceeds anything we can understand. His peace
> will guard your hearts and minds as you live in
> Christ Jesus. (Phil. 4:7)

When we find ourselves surrounded by negativity, we can intentionally limit time with negative people and influences, and instead fill our eyes and ears with things that are pleasing to God. In so doing, we build up our spiritual immune systems and enable ourselves to soak in positive influences that flow into our hearts and build our characters.

> Don't be fooled by those who say such things, for "bad company corrupts good character." (1 Cor. 15:33)

> Your eye is like a lamp that provides light for your body. When your eye is healthy, your whole body is filled with light. (Matt. 6:22)

Instead of seeing ourselves as victims, we can reject this lie, praying that God will help us choose to live in the victory He offers to all of His children. We can claim the following truths, which promise victory and freedom.

> But thanks be to God! He gives us the victory through our Lord Jesus Christ. (1 Cor. 15:57 NIV)

> For the Lord is the Spirit, and wherever the Spirit of the Lord is, there is freedom. (2 Cor. 3:17)

When we experience a loss in our life or feel like we have nothing to hope for, we can pick up the sword of truth and remember this life-giving promise from God.

> "For I know the plans I have for you," says the LORD. "They are plans for good and not for disaster, to give you a future and a hope." (Jer. 29:11)

At one time or another, I have found myself swirling in all of these sinking thought patterns and had to seek God's intervention to help me fight the battles going on in my mind. The truth is, life will always present opportunities to sink, but God is always waiting with an outstretched hand to pull us back up and renew our minds time and time again.

All Things Can Be Made New

Perhaps today you find yourself struggling with a few, or maybe even all, of these temptations. Maybe you're feeling weighted down because of the perception of broken dreams and the feeling that all is lost and nothing can ever be good again. Maybe you've always dreamed of being a mommy but struggle with infertility. Or perhaps you lost a loved one too soon and feel robbed of the future you had envisioned. Maybe a dream job ended up not working out as expected or the purchase transaction for a dream home fell through. Perhaps you long to be married but you're still looking for your soul mate.

When we experience the loss of a dream, or find ourselves trapped in the captivity of discouragement, we're vulnerable and more inclined to give in to negativity. Yet when we turn our broken dreams, broken hearts, and broken spirits over to God, He can always breathe hope back to life. Isaiah 61:3 says, "To all who mourn … he will give a crown of beauty for ashes, a joyous blessing instead of mourning, festive praise instead of despair." Optimism always opens the door for God to turn brokenness into new beginnings.

Regardless of what tempts us to think negatively, when we commit to thinking differently than we have in the past, we open the door for God to begin doing something new and amazing in our lives. We are all capable in God's strength to overcome our habits of pessimism and discouraging thoughts. The miracle of radical change in our minds can begin when we believe God is still in the business of miracles, and when we become convinced that all things, including our minds, can be made new.

Isaiah 43:19 says, "For I am about to do something new. See, I have already begun! Do you not see it?" How much happier could our lives be if we stopped asking God *what* He wanted us to *do* and started asking Him *how* He wants us to *be*? When we let go of our old way of thinking, only then can we grab hold of the new. Trust me, friend. Anything new God offers us is going to be better than anything old we have been holding on to.

STRATEGIES FOR TRANSFORMING YOUR THINKING

Mind-Transforming Reflections

- Tracie shared about stumbling into negativity when she was scheduled to speak at a women's conference. When was the last time you were caught off guard and fell into a whirlpool? How did you stay afloat? How did God help you?

- If you fell into a whirlpool and got stuck there, what might you learn from looking back on that experience that will help you avoid that temptation in the future? What scripture could you have drawn upon to help you avoid sinking?

- When Julie was suffering from negativity and hopelessness, she fell to her knees in prayer. What are the ways you "posture" yourself in order to access God's sure rescue? How do you make yourself available to God when you notice you're sinking? Is there anything you need to surrender to God today; anything you want to be freed from that is keeping you from living with joy and peace and positive thinking?

Mind-Renewing Memory Verses

Write out the verses below in your journal, or on your notecards, and commit them to memory.

Trust in the LORD always,

for the LORD GOD is the eternal Rock.

(Isa. 26:4)

The LORD is my rock, my fortress, and my

savior;

my God is my rock, in whom I find

protection.

He is my shield, the power that saves me,

and my place of safety. (Ps. 18:2)

Stay alert! Watch out for your great enemy, the devil. He prowls around like a roaring lion, looking for someone to devour. (1 Pet. 5:8)

For I am about to do something new.

See, I have already begun! Do you not see it?

I will make a pathway through the wilderness.

I will create rivers in the dry wasteland.

(Isa. 43:19)

I'll show up and take care of you as I promised and bring you back home. I know what I'm doing. I have it all planned out—plans to take care of you, not abandon you, plans to give you the future you hope for. (Jer. 29:10–11 THE MESSAGE)

Chapter Challenge

Consider the ten most common whirlpools of negative thinking that Tracie talked about in this chapter.

1. Comparison
2. "Awfulizing"
3. Exaggerating
4. Complaining
5. Blaming
6. Self-Condemnation
7. Overthinking
8. Negative Influences
9. Victim Mentality
10. All-Is-Lost Mind-Set

For each one, think of a situation when you struggled with that line of thinking. If you failed to recognize what was happening, write down how your attitude and thoughts affected that experience. Then record how that experience might have turned out differently had you let go of the anchor of negativity and anchored your heart and mind in prayer and Scripture instead. How might you have felt differently and acted differently?

Now rank the above list from one to ten in order of which whirlpool you are most likely to succumb to. Which three whirlpools do you struggle with the most? Consider copying the verse Tracie has offered above for each of these, or prayerfully ask God to show you three verses that will be particularly meaningful and applicable to you. Master these three verses. Write them on a bookmark to tuck into your Bible. Use a Sharpie to write them on your checkbook cover. Buy a bracelet or charm that portrays the verses you've chosen. Speak them out loud each day. Meditate on them. Sing them! These are God's good gift to you—they will help you stay afloat!

If you don't like something, change it.
If you can't change it, change your attitude.

Maya Angelou

Chapter Ten

OPERATION PERSEVERANCE
Keeping Your Head Above Water

*As we think, so will we be. When we change
our minds, we'll change our lives.*

In *Switch On Your Brain*, Dr. Caroline Leaf wrote: "When you understand the power of your thought life, you truly begin to get a glimpse of how important it is to take responsibility for what you are thinking…. Thinking is a powerful creative force, both a blessing and a curse, and should not be taken lightly."[1] Like me, you may have been taking the power of your thought life all too lightly, inadvertently allowing your thoughts to take you in negative directions. If God has convicted your heart with the message of this book, know that He is not only showing you a need for change, but He has also equipped you to make the change.

But let's face it. Even when we are trying our best to be more positive and optimistic, it's easy for our thoughts and emotions to trip us up. Even when we're feeling positive and calm, without warning we can find ourselves in a whirlpool because of an unexpected adversity. The truth is, it takes only seconds to find ourselves drowning under the weight of worry, with negativity pouring into the hull of our minds. But the good news is that it takes only seconds to ask God to help us get our heads back above water. Positive thinking is always just one thought away.

The choices we make about which thoughts we allow and which we reject will drive our attitude and dictate our overall happiness. When we commit to putting into practice the three steps outlined in this book—noticing negative thoughts, rejecting them, and replacing them with new thoughts—we take control of our thinking and our overall health and happiness. That's a lot of power God has put at our disposal!

Women Who Refused to Sink

Let me tell you about three women who put these steps into practice and developed unsinkable attitudes, and unsinkable faith as a result.

Aracelis's only child was leaving for college. Although it was an exciting time, normal maternal worry weighed down her enthusiasm. Rather than let those thoughts fill her with anxiousness and keep her from enjoying the opportunity to help her son prepare for this new season of life, she chose to apply the three practical steps.

> 1. She immediately noticed her negative thoughts and how her worry was taking her mind to what-if scenarios that would probably never even happen yet filled her with fear and anxiety.

2. She rejected her worries and cast them on God.

3. She replaced her negative thoughts with positive hope and trust, clinging specifically to God's truth found in Jeremiah 29:11: "'For I know the plans I have for you,' says the LORD. 'They are plans for good and not for disaster, to give you a future and a hope.'" Aracelis trusted God's plan for her and her son's lives and prayed for the Lord's protection over her son, while asking for Him to give her peace and freedom from anxiousness.

As this loving mom focused on believing God had great plans for her son, and entrusted him into God's care, she was able to let go of her worry and fill her mind with positive thoughts and hopeful feelings. As a result of her decision to take control over her thoughts, she was able to swim in faith instead of sink in negativity.

In a similar way, Suzanne found herself struggling with negative thoughts about her ex-husband's girlfriend, regarding the way she acted at times around Suzanne's grown children. Rather than let these thoughts cause turmoil in her own heart and mind, and friction within her family, she chose to apply the three practical steps.

1. She noticed her negative thoughts and how they were making her feel and act.

2. She rejected her negative thoughts, recognizing the damage they could cause internally in her heart and externally in her relationships with her children and their father.

3. She replaced them with positive thoughts about favorable things this woman has done for her children over the years, and focused on her positive attributes instead. She clung to God's truth in Philippians 4:8, "Fix your thoughts on what is true, and honorable, and right, and pure, and lovely, and admirable. Think about things that are excellent and worthy of praise."

As Suzanne focused on pleasing thoughts and character traits about this woman, which was probably not easy, instead of brooding opinions and negativity, her heart softened and her mind calmed. As a result, her thoughts didn't control her or the outcome, and she was able to swim in faith instead of sink in negativity. When she applied three simple steps to choose her thoughts, Suzanne stayed afloat. And so did her family relationships.

Kayla and I became friends online through a series of divinely ordained circumstances. Although we lived across the country from each other and had never met in person, she became an inspiration to me. Kayla and her husband and children faced many difficult adversities: living paycheck to paycheck, experiencing sudden unemployment, and even going through a short season of homelessness. Yet, through all these hardships, Kayla's attitude and her faith never wavered.

Shortly after her family got back on their feet, another storm blew in to Kayla's life with a vengeance. She was diagnosed with a brain tumor and needed immediate surgery, and was faced with a life-altering choice. She could choose to think negatively and become consumed with pessimistic, fear-filled thoughts about the future. Or she could choose to reject those negative thoughts and replace them with thoughts that would help her stay positive and lean against the One who could give her hope and get her through this hard and scary journey. She chose the latter.

> 1. Kayla noticed the temptation to be negative. Lots of people in her situation would be negative. But instead of caving into despair and negativity, she actively took her thoughts captive to Christ by trusting in God's great love for her and held on tightly to the anchor of hope.
> 2. Kayla rejected negative thoughts. Even when doctors and nurses delivered dire prognoses, she chose not to let their words sink her attitude, hope, or faith.
> 3. Kayla intentionally replaced negative thoughts with positive ones and focused on God's promises. She made her faith, the Bible, prayer, and her family a priority in her life while enlisting the prayers of her friends and loved ones as well.

With each update Kayla posted online and in emails she would occasionally send me, I saw a miracle happening. Not only the miracle of her physical healing and recovery, but also the miracle God was doing in her heart as He equipped her to push through the pain, debilitating side effects, and countless temptations to drown in the negative current of her circumstances. Instead of being angry and negative or mad at God, Kayla focused her thoughts on giving Him the glory. She temporarily lost her voice as a side effect of surgery, but she felt blessed that she could voice her faith through her writing. She lost her ability to do certain things or enjoy the taste of certain foods but constantly expressed hope and joy, believing that God would somehow use her to shine as a light for Him into the lives of others. She developed an acute sense of gratitude and thankfulness to God for the simple things in life, such as the ability to see the sun come up in the morning, remembering how to cook eggs for breakfast for her children, and the ability to do a load of laundry. Kayla offered her thoughts to God, and He blessed her with a transformed mind, a lightened heart, and a changed life.

One of her posts in particular blessed me and touched my heart:

> I serve a God who loves me each and every day, whose mercies are new each day, and whose faithfulness is beyond what you can imagine. I'm grateful for what I am going through each and every moment—the pain and all—because it leads me to turn to my Father who is right next

to me holding my hand so gently, but at the same
time so tightly, that I can feel His hand pressed
against my own.

What a beautiful example of unsinkable faith and optimism!
Kayla didn't allow her trials and setbacks to sink her attitude or
trap her in a whirlpool of negativity. Instead, she lived acutely
aware of noticing, rejecting, and replacing negative thoughts on a
daily basis. Her positive mind-set was just as critical to her health
and healing as were the treatments for her condition.

As we think, so will we be. Thoughts are powerful. They determine not only our happiness in the present but also our hope for
the future, and our destiny down the road.

Refuse to Give In to Negativity

The Mayo Clinic posted this thought, "Positive thinking doesn't
mean that you keep your head in the sand and ignore life's less
pleasant situations. Positive thinking just means that you approach
unpleasantness in a more positive and productive way. You think
the best is going to happen, not the worst."[2] While this statement
is uplifting, it's easier said than done!

It's not realistic to think we'll never feel discouraged or negative, because as stated in John 16:33, "Here on earth you will
have many trials and sorrows." God doesn't expect us to keep our
heads in the sand and just pretend problems or negativity don't
exist. He has given us the God-tools and the power of the Holy

Spirit within us to transform our hearts and minds to be more like Him. In His strength, we can renew our minds to always try to think the best, instead of the worst. If we are willing to persevere, positive thinking can become a habit we will never want to break.

You will be successful in thinking positively if you implement a strategy that works, like the three steps to help you take charge of your thoughts. You will be strengthened with the tools God offers: Scripture and prayer. You'll avoid failure when you learn to navigate dangerous whirlpools. You'll be encouraged when you realize the success of journeying with an accountability partner. Hear me: you can have the kind of satisfying and joy-filled life you desire when you choose to make it happen.

It CAN Happen for You

I wish I'd known sooner that when I invited God to change my thoughts that my life would be changed as well. How much happier I could have been had I not spent so many years listening to self-condemning thoughts, allowing difficult circumstances and people to steal my joy, and losing hope and peace when problems seemed out of my control. I can't get that time back or change the past, nor can you. But I can enjoy unsinkable faith, joy, peace, and hope in the future if I intentionally pursue a life grounded in God's truths and strive for a positive outlook and attitude, even on the hardest of days.

If you've been mired in negativity for years, it may feel impossible to change. But, sweet friend, nothing is impossible with Christ. A habit of positive thinking and a transformed, renewed mind is possible for every one of His children. If you passionately want to be *up*, nothing can make you be *down* without your permission. The only way to find out how optimism and positivity can change your life is to commit to having a positive attitude and to entertain positive thoughts. You have the power to make that choice, and when you do, your life will never be the same again.

Life is not always as we think it should be, but it is always as God planned it to be. He is in control, and we are not, but He is always holding out the holy life preserver to rescue us from despair, negativity, hopelessness, and joylessness. I love the hopeful promises we see in Psalm 40:1–3:

> I waited patiently for the LORD to help me,
>> and he turned to me and heard my cry.
> He lifted me out of the pit of despair,
>> out of the mud and the mire.
> He set my feet on solid ground
>> and steadied me as I walked along.
> He has given me a new song to sing,
>> a hymn of praise to our God.
> Many will see what he has done and be amazed.
>> They will put their trust in the LORD.

When we seek Him, we will find Him, and if we ask for rescue, we will find rescue. God is longing to put a new song in your heart today—a sweet song that bubbles up from your thoughts and flows from your lips for all to hear.

My Heart for You

Oh, precious friend, the cry of my heart is that you will discover the joy of a transformed and renewed mind. You can be free. You don't have to feel the way you've been feeling or live the way you've been living. You can experience joy. Transformation is possible. I know because I have experienced it. The same holy power that rescued and equipped me and all the other women mentioned in this book to transform our minds and redirect our lives in a positive direction is the same power available in you.

My prayer is that, despite how long you've been bound by negativity, and regardless of the difficult circumstances, thoughts, and emotions you've been struggling with, you can now see the benefit of a positive outlook and have latched on to the hope that it is possible. A heart and mind grounded in Christ can stand firm when the storms of life roll in, and an attitude of hope, joy, and optimism will always help us keep our heads above water. When our thought life becomes unsinkable, our faith will too.

As we think, my friend, so will we be. When you change your mind, you'll change your life.

STRATEGIES FOR TRANSFORMING YOUR THINKING

Mind-Transforming Reflections

- What is one situation in your life today—something you're actually facing this week—where you can apply the three practical steps and make those thoughts captive to Christ? Explore that particular situation in your journal and visualize the freedom that's possible.

  1. Notice your thoughts and how they are making you feel and act.
  2. Reject negative thoughts and refuse to believe them.
  3. Replace negative thoughts with positive thoughts instead, thoughts that align with the words of God.

- Throughout this book we've considered Romans 12:2, "Don't copy the behavior and customs of this world, but let God transform you into a new person by changing the way you think." As you continue to practice capturing your thoughts, it will become more natural. God's heart is for you to experience change and new life. How has that begun to happen in your heart and mind? List any changes you've already seen in your life. Also, write a prayer seeking God's intervention in the areas you want to change. Pour out gratitude for what He has already done to help you transform your mind, and seek His strength and power to continue making negative thinking and a negative life things of the past.

Mind-Renewing Memory Verses

Write out the verses below in your journal, or on your notecards, and commit them to memory.

> Praise the LORD!
> Give thanks to the LORD, for he is good!
> His faithful love endures forever. (Ps. 106:1)

> Patient endurance is what you need now, so that you will continue to do God's will. Then you will receive all that he has promised. (Heb. 10:36)

> Fix your thoughts on what is true, and honorable, and right, and pure, and lovely, and admirable. Think about things that are excellent and worthy of praise. (Phil. 4:8)

> For God has not given us a spirit of fear and timidity, but of *power*, love, and self-discipline. (2 Tim. 1:7)

Restore to me the joy of your salvation,
and let a willing attitude control me.
(Ps. 51:12 ISV)

Chapter Challenge

For the next twenty-one days, commit to finding something positive in every situation, no matter how bleak or negative it seems. Each time you find yourself thinking a negative thought, immediately think of something positive about what you're facing. If you find yourself in an unpleasant or difficult situation, identify at least one thing that could be positive about that situation.

For example, if you're upset about something that happened in your workplace, bring to mind tangible and intangible benefits of working there and ponder those instead. If someone says something that hurts your feelings, consider how that experience might drive you into God's Word and help you learn a new verse about God's love and acceptance of you. If you're just having a bad day and feel downtrodden or frustrated, look for something to be happy about in the midst of your discouragement and shift your thinking to that instead. This will not be an easy feat—but then again, challenges are never easy.

When we challenge ourselves to think positively, we are taking the wheels of our lives and steering them in the direction we want to go. Intentionally focusing on being more positive for a period of twenty-one days straight will help you learn to enjoy life in the moment, no matter what life presents. Once you've completed the first twenty-one days of the challenge, turn the calendar and start again. Habits take time to form, but forming positive habits can be one of the greatest gifts we ever give ourselves.

When we form a habit of looking for the good in life, instead of the bad, it leads to unsinkable peace, joy, happiness, and—most of all—unsinkable faith.

For as [she] thinks in [her] heart, so is [she].

Proverbs 23:7 AMP

ACKNOWLEDGMENTS

To Alice Crider, my senior acquisitions and development editor, and everyone at David C Cook publishing: I can't thank you enough for your patience, compassion, and support over the past couple of years. Your continued kindness, understanding, and willingness to be flexible when needed in so many ways far exceeded what any author could have ever asked for or expected. The understanding and kindness you've shown before, during, and after the process of writing *Unsinkable Faith* is surely unprecedented. Thank you for not only giving me the opportunity to work with David C Cook, but for having unwavering faith in me and my writing. I will be forever grateful for the grace you extended to me throughout this process, and I am honored to work with such amazing people at such an amazing organization.

To Margot Starbuck, my independent editor: This book could not have been written without your help. Your enthusiasm for your work, and for mine, helped push me through difficult days of writing when the task and the goal seemed impossible. Your outgoing personality, great ideas, and positive encouragement were a true blessing, and helped bring to life the message God laid on my heart. I'm so thankful our paths crossed. Thank you for everything you did.

To Greg Johnson, my agent at WordServe Literary Group: Your continued concern and kindness for me over the years, as a person and not just a client, has not gone unnoticed. Thank you for not only keeping in touch with me while this book was being written, but for your ongoing genuine compassion and support. I so appreciate all your kind words of encouragement and for always being willing to brainstorm and toss around ideas with me. I am thankful for you and know that with you as my agent, I will always have a faithful supporter and friend who derives true joy in helping others succeed.

To my three children, Morgan, Kaitlyn, and Michael: There is absolutely no way I would have made it through our difficult season of life—much less been able to write this book—without your love, support, and friendship. You believed in me and encouraged me, even when I didn't believe in myself, and graciously put up with all my crazy emotions while juggling your own. On so many occasions when the load felt too heavy, you each gently reminded me of God's simple promises in your own ways, which brought more joy to my heart as a mom than you'll ever realize. You are strong and loving, and awesome young adults of which I'm blessed to call mine.

To Barbara, my mother: You have exuded an optimistic attitude my entire life, even while enduring countless hardships and adversities. You are a true example of how one's attitude determines their destiny and their happiness, not their circumstances. Your unconditional love and selflessness toward anyone you have ever known, and your unwavering ability to think positive, is a legacy not many people can claim. Thank you for raising me to love Jesus, for always being a godly role model, for inspiring me to live a life of optimism, and for teaching me that joy is a choice.

To every one of my precious girlfriends from Pine Lake Country Club and all my incredible Proverbs 31 sisters, who, aside from Jesus, have been my lifeline: Your loyalty, compassion, and unconditional love have meant more to me than you will ever know. Your devoted friendship, godly advice and wisdom, constant support, prayers and encouragement, and all our laughter and fun times together have filled my life with more joy than I can express. You continually helped me be strong when I felt weak and lifted me up when I was down, even if you didn't realize the impact you were having on my heart and my spirit. I've always heard a person is blessed if they have one or two true friends in life, and I have been blessed with more amazing, faithful, precious friends than any one person deserves. You all know who you are—thank you.

NOTES

Chapter One: Your Feelings Aren't the Boss of You

1. "Norman Vincent Peale Quotes," BrainyQuote, accessed November 2, 2016, www.brainyquote.com/quotes/authors/n/norman_vincent_peale.html.

Chapter Two: Tens of Thousands of Reasons

1. Jennifer Read Hawthorn, "Change Your Thoughts, Change Your World," Words to Live By, accessed November 2, 2016, www.jenniferhawthorne .com/articles/change_your_thoughts.html.

2. Bruce Davis, "There Are 50,000 Thoughts Standing between You and Your Partner Every Day!," *Huffington Post*, May 23, 2013, www.huffingtonpost .com/bruce-davis-phd/healthy-relationships_b_3307916.html.

3. "Don't Believe Everything You Think," Cleveland Clinic Wellness, accessed November 2, 2016, www.clevelandclinicwellness.com/programs/NewSFN /pages/default.aspx?Lesson=3&Topic=2&UserId=00000000-0000-0000 -0000-000000000705.

Chapter Three: Count the Cost

1. "Naomi," Behind the Name, accessed November 2, 2016, www.behindthename .com/name/naomi-1.

2. "Mara," Behind the Name, accessed November 2, 2016, www.behindthename .com/name/mara-1.

3. Caroline Leaf, *Switch On Your Brain: The Key to Peak Happiness, Thinking, and Health* (Grand Rapids, MI: Baker, 2013), 32.

4. Leaf, *Switch On Your Brain*, 32.

Chapter Five: Breaking the Habit

1. Joyce Meyer, *Battlefield of the Mind: Winning the Battle in Your Mind* (Nashville: FaithWords, 1995), 147.

2. Phillippa Lally, et. al, "How Are Habits Formed: Modelling Habit Formation in the Real World," *European Journal of Social Psychology*, July 16, 2009, http://onlinelibrary.wiley.com/doi/10.1002/ejsp.674/abstract.

3. Elliott Berkman, quoted in Signe Dean, "Here's How Long It Takes to Break a Habit, according to Science," Science Alert, September 24, 2015, www.sciencealert.com/here-s-how-long-it-takes-to-break-a-habit-according-to-science.

4. Daniel G. Amen, *Change Your Brain, Change Your Life: The Breakthrough Program for Conquering Anxiety, Depression, Obsessiveness, Lack of Focus, Anger, and Memory Problems* (New York: Harmony Books, 1998), 27.

5. Amen, *Change Your Brain*, 52.

6. Meyer, *Battlefield*, 44.

7. Amen, *Change Your Brain*, 118.

Chapter Six: Row, Row, Row Your Boat

1. Joyce Meyer, *Battlefield of the Mind: Winning the Battle in Your Mind* (Nashville: FaithWords, 1995), 261.

2. Daniel G. Amen, *Change Your Brain, Change Your Life: The Breakthrough Program for Conquering Anxiety, Depression, Obsessiveness, Lack of Focus, Anger, and Memory Problems* (New York: Harmony Books, 1998), 111.

3. Ralph P. Martin, "2 Corinthians," in *Word Biblical Commentary*, vol. 40 (Waco, TX: Word Books, 1986), 306.

Chapter Seven: Instruments No Crew Member Should Be Without

1. Ralph P. Martin, "2 Corinthians," in *Word Biblical Commentary*, vol. 40 (Waco, TX: Word Books, 1986), 306.

2. Charles Capps, *The Tongue, a Creative Force* (London: Capps, 1995), 1–2, 6.

3. Capps, *Tongue*, 23.

4. Caroline Leaf, *Switch On Your Brain: The Key to Peak Happiness, Thinking, and Health* (Grand Rapids, MI: Baker, 2013), 73.

5. Abbey Wedgeworth, "Praise for My Postpartum Body," Gentle Leading, June 6, 2016, www.gentleleading.com/blog/2016/6/5/praise-for-my -postpartum-body.

6. For more information, see www.corysproject.com.

Chapter Eight: Mayday, Mayday!

1. Alan Ryden, "Miracle Rescue in Alaska—a Powerful Testimony of Survival and Strength," Elijah List, February 16, 2008, www.elijahlist.com/words /display_word.html?ID=6170.

2. Ryden, "Miracle."

3. Charles H. Dyer, "Lamentations," in *The Bible Knowledge Commentary: Old Testament*, ed. John F. Walvoord and Roy B. Zuck (Wheaton, IL: Victor Books, 1985), 1207.

4. Dictionary.com, s.v. "paradigm shift," accessed November 2, 2016, www.dictionary.com/browse/paradigm-shift.

Chapter Ten: Operation Perseverance

1. Caroline Leaf, *Switch On Your Brain: The Key to Peak Happiness, Thinking, and Health* (Grand Rapids, MI: Baker, 2013), 124.

2. "Positive Thinking: Stop Negative Self-Talk to Reduce Stress," Mayo Clinic, March 4, 2014, www.mayoclinic.org/healthy-lifestyle/stress-management /in-depth/positive-thinking/art-20043950.

BIBLE CREDITS

The author has added italics to Scripture quotations for emphasis.

ABOUT THE AUTHOR

Bestselling author Tracie Miles has been a member of the Proverbs 31 national speaker and writer teams since 2006. She is a monthly contributor to the Proverbs 31 Ministries' *Encouragement for Today* daily email devotions, which have an estimated reach of well over one million people per day. She is also a contributing author to the popular Zondervan *NIV Women's Devotional Bible* and the *Encouragement for Today* daily devotional book.

Tracie travels across the country to share encouragement from God for everyday living and inspire women to live a life of joy, peace, and purpose. Check out her speaking schedule or inquire about bringing her to speak at your church women's event at http://traciemiles.com/speaking.

Stay connected with Tracie:

Facebook: www.facebook.com/p31traciemiles

Twitter: www.twitter.com/traciewmiles

Instagram: www.instagram.com/traciemiles

Pinterest: www.pinterest.com/traciewmiles

www.traciemiles.com

OPTIMIST CHALLENGE

SIGN UP FOR THE 5 DAY OPTIMIST CHALLENGE!

 Are you ready to officially challenge yourself to be a more positive person, train your mind to think like a hope-filled optimist, and live life with more joy and peace? Put the truths and principles found in this book into practice in your everyday life by taking Tracie's free bonus personal challenge series to transform your mind and life.

If you enjoyed *Unsinkable Faith* and can bear witness to the change God has already done in transforming your heart and mind, be sure to invite your friends to take the challenge with you! Remember, you have the power within you not only to transform the way you think, feel, and live but also to encourage others to do the same. We can all change and make an impact on the world we live in, one optimistic thought at a time.

Visit Tracie's blog for more information and to sign up to participate in the free 5 Day Optimist Challenge: **www.traciemiles.com**.

BLOG CHALLENGES

INTERESTED IN MORE LIFE-CHANGING RESOURCES FROM TRACIE MILES?

Visit Tracie's online store to sign up for more free email campaigns to challenge you in your faith walk, or purchase the ebook versions to complete at your own pace. You can also check out her Bible-study materials available for purchase, which accompany each of her books.

5 Day Faith Zone Challenge

This life-changing and empowering challenge offers five days of devotions, with each day providing a specific challenge for doing one thing that will help you grow closer to God and closer to discovering your divinely designed purpose, followed by a prayer for the day and challenging scriptures to ponder.

10 Day Stress Detox

This challenge gives ten thought-provoking articles to de-stressing your life by focusing on God's perspective of your stressors and allowing His suggestions for stress relief to change your heart and fill you with peace. Each daily detox article offers inspiration and encouragement for tackling one common stressor of life, in addition to a peace-filled Bible verse and a daily detox activity to help you implement biblically based stress-relief principles into your everyday life.

Also available for purchase:

> *Unsinkable Faith Participant Study Guide*
> *Unsinkable Faith Leader Guide*
> *Your Life Still Counts Participant Study Guide*
> *Your Life Still Counts Leader Guide*
> *Your Life Still Counts Video Series Bundle*
> *Stressed-Less Living Participant Study Guide*
> *Stressed-Less Living Leader Guide*

OTHER BOOKS BY TRACIE MILES

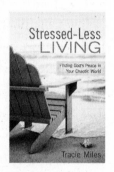

Life is stressful. The stress of dealing with work, coworkers, parenting, finances, and marriage and relationships, in addition to the stressors of politics and the economy, can sometimes make us feel like we are a pressure cooker about to explode. If we don't release some of that pressure, an explosion is inevitable. The world we live in believes stress is normal and just a part of everyday life that we have to accept and deal with, but that is not what God intends for us. Peace is possible, even in the midst of less than peaceful circumstances, if we learn to look for it in the right places.

Readers can find the peace for which they hunger in this breakthrough book, as Tracie helps women break free from the prison of unrelenting stress and learn to rely on the peace that Christ promises all those who come to Him. Tracie unpacks the truths found in Scripture about how to overcome fear, anxiety, uncertainty, and feeling overwhelmed and shows the stressed-out woman how she can not only survive stress but also thrive in spite of it through faith in the promises of God.

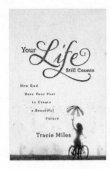

Do regret and shame over your failures, sins, and shortcomings make you wonder how you could ever be loved, much less used, by a holy God? Tracie felt the same way until she discovered the path to healing, peace, purpose, and significance. God not only has a purpose for you, but He has prepared you for your divine purpose based specifically on the experiences of your past. Those experiences that we often think disqualify us from being used in God's kingdom are actually the very things that God has used to prepare us for purpose beyond our imagination.

Through her own story and stories from other women who have discovered God's purpose for their lives specifically through their own adverse experiences and past mistakes, Tracie helps you see how God truly can turn pain into purpose and ashes into beauty. You will find forgiveness and healing from the troubles and mistakes of your past, discover the courage to step out of your comfort zone to help others find hope and strength, and be inspired to embrace the beautiful future God divinely designed for you.